# Christ in the Psalms

## Gerald L. Finneman

# Christ in the Psalms

## Gerald L. Finneman

**GLAD TIDINGS PUBLISHERS**
8784 Valley View Drive
Berrien Springs, Michigan 49103 U.S.A.

# Christ in the Psalms

**Gerald L. Finneman**

Unless otherwise indicated, Scripture is taken from the New King James Version.
Copyright © 1979, 1980, 1982 by Thomas Nelson, Inc. Used by permission. All rights reserved.
Bible texts credited to KJV are from the King James Version.

Book and cover design by Glad Tidings Publishers

PRINTED IN U.S.A.

ISBN 1-931218-74-9

[00164]

# Preface

The background leading to the writing of this book came from the requests of students and others who were helped by presentations about the mental anguish experienced by Christ as portrayed in the Psalms. Before there was a thought of putting this into a book the material was presented first in Bible studies and later in sermons. It might have stayed in those formats except for the requests and encouragement from those who wanted to see the information in written format, but not in academic obscurity.

Academic theses are usually able to focus intensely on a single topic or passage. They are the result of delving into issues that have not been explored in the past. A good thesis is able to present an extended argument systematically that thoroughly deals with all the issues relating to the topic. A thesis is written with the knowledge that it must be defended before academic scrutiny. Although this is not the scope of this book the intention is to examine carefully and in detail the Son of Man as He is presented in the Psalms.

This book will appeal especially to those who have suffered intense mental anguish, even mental breakdown. Those who have experienced emotional brokenness can understand more fully the mental torment that Jesus went through as He was "made to be sin for us" than those who have not experienced such trauma.

Not with claims of writing ability or skill is this book set forth, but it comes from a heart touched through the study and meditations of the Passion of Christ in the Psalms. It comes from a mind that went through two years of depression and despondency from which some acquaintances thought I would never recover. However, God had other plans.

Some persons who have experienced deep discouragement, despondency and despair brought on by situations beyond their control have found hope in the Passion of Christ exhibited in the Psalms.

Others by their own wrong behaviors, resulting in depression, also have found comfort from the sympathetic Savior who forgives, cleanses and restores one personally to favor with God.

There are still others who, fearful by what the Bible calls a future "time of trouble" that is certain to come upon all the inhabitants of earth, have found comfort in the fact that Christ experienced a time of trouble that no human will ever have to endure.

The Psalms point to Jesus as the only One who is able to meet the needs of the soul. The path of peace is opened to those whose feet are halting and whose minds are doubting the love of God and His personal interest in them.

There are passages in the Psalms about Jesus in which hearts have been touched most deeply, and have brought tears to the eyes of the readers because of the great love of Christ demonstrated in His sufferings for them. Healing of mind and spirit have followed.

The Passion of Christ—the sufferings of Jesus—in the period following the Last Supper and including His Crucifixion is what saves us. The physical punishment He received was terrible. However, this was not what atoned for our sins. It was the mental torture endured by Jesus, because of sin, that made atonement.

Some people are moved to sympathy for Jesus and even experience a powerful emotional upheaval when they hear a recital or see a film portraying Christ's physical sufferings. Many mistake this sympathy and emotional trauma as a conversion experience. Bible conversion effects the emotions, but it effects much more than these feelings. It brings with it a decided change in the life. Conversions comes when one responds to the working of the Holy Spirit. The unregenerate person is brought to a realization of his wretchedness and responds to the grace of God through heart-felt repentance for sin accompanied with faith in Christ.

Knowledge of the mental sufferings of Christ for us, accepted and believed, produces reformation in the life and practices. The weaker the knowledge of Christ crucified, the less clear and powerful will be our gospel witness even though the emotions have been stirred and disturbed.

It cannot but be of great importance in the interests of a thorough, sure, and comprehensive knowledge of Christ crucified that the results in progressive effort in the preaching of the everlasting gospel and in research of the study of the plan of redemption which should be mutually exchanged and spread from people to people. To this end it is my hope that this book will contribute in some small way to the present riches of the knowledge of our Savior and Lord and to the spreading of the good news of Christ as predicted in the Psalms.

*— The Author*

# Contents

# Contents

# Chapter 1

# Christ in the Psalms

The Book of Psalms is the diary of Jesus Christ, written in advance of His becoming a man. Here we find the gospel of Christ presented as definitely as in any other book of the Bible. It is all of Christ.

The various writers of the psalms recorded the common experiences of humanity. Of the experiences of mankind written in the Psalms, Christ's are paramount. The psalms mean Christ. Christ as God. Christ as man. Christ in His sufferings, His death, resurrection and ascension. The psalms deal with the truth about Jesus—the truth about Christ for us, with us, and as us. This truth is presented more clearly in the psalms than anywhere else in the Bible. Christ is the theme of the psalms.

In the psalms we see a picture of the mind and emotions of Jesus. They describe the inner workings of His thinking; what went on in His mind while He was tested and tried in various situations, especially while He was on the cross. Christ and the cross comprised the battlefield where the great controversy between right and wrong raged; where agape (God's unconditional love) and selfishness stood face-to-face in mortal combat.

The cross demonstrates that agape is greater than selfishness, that justification is greater than condemnation. That what Adam did to us was frightful, but Christ reversed both the condemnation and the direction in which the race was headed because of Adam's sin. Adam and consequently the human race within himself was headed straight for hell; but in Himself, Christ turned the entire race around and headed it toward heaven. Because of Christ, one must get off the pathway in order to not arrive in heaven.

The term "the cross" refers to Christ's entire life—it epitomizes the giving of Himself for the benefit of others. He demonstrated that righteousness is greater than transgression and that the Spirit is mightier than the flesh.

Paul took up this theme in the book of Galatians, and in Romans he wrote that grace is greater than sin. Wherever sin resides or "abounds," grace does "much more" abound in that very place (Romans 5:20). Grace and sin met at the cross, and grace was victor. Even though Christ was made to be sin, and died the equivalent of the second death, grace is still greater than sin. And faith—the faith of Jesus—is greater than unbelief.

The psalms present the battle as it was hammered out, and there we are shown several truths about the cross and what it means to us:

• The cross was considered the curse of God, but out of that curse came blessing—blessing to the human race.

• In the cross Christ was made to be sin, that we might be made the righteousness of God in Him.

• The cross was nothing but condemnation to the human race. But Christ took that condemnation so that we might be justified.

• In the cross we find eternal life—the opposite of the second death. Out of that death came life for the human race, especially for those who believe. Whatever Satan did to us through sin, God did something much more, as demonstrated by the cross of Christ.

When Jesus met with His disciples after the resurrection, He explained the Old Testament Scriptures to them. He studied specifically the psalms concerning His sufferings, death and resurrection (Luke 24:44-46). Earlier in His ministry He stated that the Old Testament testified of Him (John 5:39). The Old Testament is to be studied in the light of the life of Christ. If one refuses to believe that the Old Testament testifies of Christ, then he cannot believe the New Testament (John 5:46, 47).

When Christ was on the cross, He spoke what are known as the seven last words. The first three concern Christ's relationship with others, the last four are about His union with His heavenly Father. These are listed here for consideration:

- "Father, forgive them, for they do not know what they do" (Luke 23:34).
- "Assuredly, I say to you today, you will be with Me in Paradise" (Luke 23:43).
- "Woman, behold you son!" and to John: "Behold you mother!" (John 19:26, 27).
- "My God, My God, why have You forsaken Me!" (Matthew 27:46).
- "I thirst" (John 19:28).
- "It is finished" (John 19:30).
- "Father, into Your hands I commit My spirit" (Luke 23:46).

Christ's first word from the cross was a prayer for forgiveness: "Father forgive them, for they know not what they do" (Luke 23:34). This was in behalf of those who placed Him on the cross driving the nails through His hands and feet. That prayer was not merely for Roman soldiers. We too were there. Unknowingly, corporate humanity crucified Jesus. Our sins shot the sharper pain into His heart. His prayer includes us.

This prayer must have affected the thief on the cross, for in the attitude of Christ he saw the love of God. He may have heard of Christ earlier in life, but he turned away through the influence of associates. Now, on his cross, he had nothing left and finally cried out, "Lord remember me when You come into Your kingdom." Jesus replied: "I say to you today, you will be with Me in Paradise" (Luke 23:40-43).

The first part of the day, Christ's mother Mary was taken away. She was weakened to see her Son suffer that way. We don't know if she realized that this was a fulfillment of what the prophet Simeon had said, that a sword would pierce through her own soul (Luke 2:34, 35).

John was always in the background. He recognized the telltale signs of death. Death was coming more rapidly than usual. (Crucifixions were designed to cause excruciating pain for several days before the crucified one finally gave up and died.) John recognized that Jesus was dying, so he brought Mary back to the cross. When Jesus saw her standing with John at the foot of the cross, He first spoke to Mary, "Woman, behold your son!" And then to John, "Behold your mother!" ["This is your mother now, take care of her."] (John 19:26, 27). This was a sacred blessing that came to John in those closing hours of the life of the Savior of the world, to be able to have Mary spend the rest of her life under his care.

The last four sayings of Christ came directly from the Psalms. Unlike the first three, these four are not concerned about others. Christ was now entering into His time of extreme agony, as He began to feel the separation between Himself and His Father. We read in Psalm 22:1, "My God, My God, why have You forsaken Me?" The New Testament presents it as, "Eloi, eloi, lama sabachthani?" (Mark 15:34).

Later Christ said, "I thirst" (John 19:28). This is based on Psalm 69:21, which states that He would be given gall for food and vinegar to drink.

The next statement of Jesus is recorded in John 19:30 where He says, "It is finished!" This is from Psalm 22:31, meaning that He has done or accomplished the work He was sent to do.

In Psalm 22 we observe the agony of separation that occurred between Christ and His heavenly Father. Then He died with these words on His lips, "Father, 'into Your hands I commend My spirit'" (Luke 23:46), a quotation from Psalm 31:5. During the entire closing hours on the cross, Christ quoted from the Psalms. He must have lived by the Psalms, and then died by them.

## Psalm 22 shows Christ living by faith from His birth.

"You are He who took Me out of the womb; You made Me trust when I was on My mother's breasts. I was cast upon You from birth. From My mother's womb You have been My God" (verses 9, 10). From the time of His birth until He died, Christ lived by faith in the power of God's keeping care. Just as we learn by faith (Hebrews 11:3), so did Christ learn by faith.

He was sanctified by faith through the truth as we must be sanctified by it. John 17:19 records this concerning Jesus, "I sanctify Myself, that they [the disciples] also may be sanctified by the truth." Sanctification is always connected with faith (Acts 26:18). There is only one thing Jesus did not do by faith, and that was to die. He did however die in faith, just as it is recorded of others in the book of Hebrews (11:13) who are said to have died in faith.

The Father made promises to the Son that He would keep Him from falling. These are from the everlasting covenant and are recorded in Isaiah and in the Psalms (Isaiah 49: 8, 9; 50:4-7; Psalm 22:9, 10). The testimony of Jesus is that He, the Son, could do nothing of Himself: "The Father who dwells in Me does the works" (John 14:10). In the Psalms, in Luke, and in Hebrews, we learn that needed grace was given to Christ (Psalm 45:2; Luke 2:40, 52). According to Hebrews 2:9, it was by grace that He tasted death for everyone.

## Our guiding principle in the study of the psalms.

It must be this: to see that they are the revelation of Jesus Christ. David who wrote most of the psalms was not only the father–ancestor of Christ's humanity, but he was also a type of Christ. The psalms were given for the supreme purpose of revealing Christ and His salvation. The Spirit of God, in the New Testament, applied many of the psalms to Christ so there can be no question that they refer to Him. When we read these we know we are reading of Christ. He was made to

be sin for us. All the sins and guilt and condemnation of mankind were laid upon Him. Of this the psalms speak.

Psalm 2 is the first that specifically speaks about Jesus.
It is prophetic of Him. Here we learn about the opposition of
the ungodly against Christ. A battle for freedom that is opposed to God is recorded here. Warnings and entreaties are
given. A triumphant Christ is here predicted. It is also a song
in which people deride God and His Messiah. Here also we
observe a literary device in which David reveals God mocking
the people, even as they mock Him.

The psalm begins, "Why do the nations rage, and the
people plot a vain thing?" This is quoted in Acts 4:25 by the
Apostles concerning Christ's crucifixion. The psalm continues:

> "The kings of the earth set themselves, and
> the rulers take counsel together, against the
> Lord and against His Anointed, saying, 'Let us
> break Their bonds in pieces and cast away Their
> cords from us.' He who sits in the heavens shall
> laugh; the Lord shall hold them in derision.
> Then He shall speak to them in His wrath, and
> distress them in His deep displeasure: 'Yet I have
> set My King on My holy hill of Zion. I will declare
> the decree: the Lord has said to Me, "You are My
> Son, Today I have begotten You. Ask of Me, and
> I will give You the nations for Your inheritance,
> and the ends of the earth for Your possession.
> You shall break them with a rod of iron; You
> shall dash them in pieces like a potter's vessel."'
> Now therefore, be wise, O kings; be instructed,
> you judges of the earth. Serve the Lord with fear,
> and rejoice with trembling. Kiss the Son, lest He
> be angry ..."

The term "kiss the Son" refers to an act of homage, respect, and worship. Psalm 2 also points to Christ's connection
with David in rulership. When David was anointed king, he

did not assume the kingship immediately. He always believed that Saul was "the anointed of the Lord." David had at least two opportunities to end Saul's life, but he refused to do so. Even when David cut off a piece of Saul's garment on one occasion, he was conscience-smitten and apologized for what he had done.

When Saul died, David even then did not fully take over the rulership of Judah—not until the people asked him to rule over them. That is the way it is with the Lord Jesus Christ. He waits for us to ask Him to rule over us individually and as a corporate body of believers. Christ's rulership will be because His people want Him, not because He forces Himself upon them. He then will rule with His "shepherd's rod." Most of the time the shepherd's rod was used for protection, but it was also used for discipline when needed. The rulership of Jesus will be very much like that of His ancestor David; there will be discipline, but also protection.

"I will declare the decree: The Lord has said to Me, 'You are My Son, Today I have begotten You. Ask of Me, and I will give You the nations for Your inheritance, and the ends of the earth for Your possession'" (verses 7, 8).

Paul quoting verse 7 applies this begetting of Christ to the good news of His resurrection from the dead: "And we declare to you the glad tidings—that promise which was made to the fathers. God has fulfilled this for us their children, in that He has raised up Jesus. As it is also written in the second psalm: 'You are My son, today I have begotten You'" (Acts 13:32, 33).

Paul here also quotes Psalm 16:10: "You will not allow Your Holy One to see corruption." Because Christ underwent no decay in the grave, but rather was raised from the dead, Paul concluded: "Therefore let it be known to you, brethren, that through this Man is preached to you the forgiveness of sins; and by Him everyone who believes is justified from all things" (Acts 13:38, 39). Earlier Peter had quoted Psalm 16 in his sermon at Pentecost, which is a promise from God to

Christ concerning His resurrection (Acts 2:25-31). We will consider further this psalm later.

Let's now turn to a trilogy of psalms, three literary works, related in subject and theme of tragedy and triumph.

# Chapter 2

## The Death, Burial and Resurrection, and Ascension Psalms

## Psalms 22, 23, and 24

Psalm 22 is known as the Calvary or Golgotha psalm. Psalm 23 is the burial and resurrection psalm, followed by the ascension psalm in chapter 24. Psalms 23 and 24 also reflect the second Advent.

Psalm 22 begins with the piercing cry that Christ in agony screamed as His heart broke from the burden of sin: "My God, My God, why have You forsaken Me?" It ends with "It is finished." Here we are shown the sufferings and death of Christ.

Psalm 22 is the Crucifixion Psalm. In it are recorded the thoughts of Christ's mind during the time He hung on the cross, particularly from the time when He felt forsaken of God until He exclaimed, "It is finished." This psalm ends in triumph. The last few words come from one word in the original: "finished." This word is one of the last spoken by the crucified Christ on Calvary: "It is finished!"

In Psalm 23, probably the best known psalm in the world, we think of Jesus as the Shepherd. But He was also the Lamb—the Lamb who takes away the sin of the world. The twenty-third psalm is a picture of Christ the Lamb of God depending on *His* Shepherd. Every lamb needs a shepherd. Jesus was no exception. Read the psalm with this in mind: Christ, the Lamb; His Father, the Shepherd:

1. "The Lord is My Shepherd; I shall not want.

2. "He makes Me to lie down in green pastures; He leads Me beside the still waters.

3. "He restores My soul; He leads Me in the paths of righteousness for His name's sake.

4. "Yea, though I walk through the valley of the shadow of death, I will fear no evil; for You are with me [the reason we can walk this path is because Jesus walked it before us]; Your rod and Your staff, they comfort Me [He was comforted by God's rod and staff—both discipline and guidance].

5. "You prepare a table before Me in the presence of My enemies; You anoint My head with oil; My cup runs over.

6. "Surely goodness and mercy shall follow Me all the days of My life; and I will dwell in the house of the Lord forever."

This psalm must have been a very precious promise to the Lord Jesus Christ when He walked this earth as a mortal man. In verse 4 we see the faith of Jesus. His *feelings* were that God had separated from Him, but He says, "I know that You *are* with Me," I know that You are going through this with Me. Then in verse 6, we are shown the idea of the resurrection when He says that He knows He will "dwell in the house of the Lord forever." His faith was based on the Word of God—that God would bring Him through both death and the grave.

## We have evidence that a dead Christ was more powerful than a living devil.

It was impossible for the devil to keep Christ in his prison house, the tomb. We read in Revelation 1:18 that Christ now "has the keys of Hades and of Death." He took away the keys from the devil and unlocked the grave in behalf of the human race. The grave was the devil's prison, but Christ burst the tomb. The devil could not keep Him there. Christ demonstrated that even in that place of death He was stronger than the devil. How much more now the power of the living Christ is an encouragement to us!

Christ demonstrated that He had power over death and the grave by defying death. He did so by entering into its realm. He took death upon Himself by laying down His life, then taking it up again by His Father's authority (Acts 2:23, 24; John 10:17, 18). This was because of His sinless life. Sin spent its entire force upon Him, and it did not mar Him in the least. It did not make a single blot on His character. His life was sinless, and because of this, the grave and death could have no power over Him.

That same life is given to us when we believe on the Son of God. There is victory in this belief—victory over the grave, and victory now in this present life. We give our sins to the Lord our Savior, and we take His sinless life in their place.

### "I shall not want."

All of Christ's needs were met. There is a difference between needs and desires. His desire, however strong, was never allowed to dominate His submission to the Father's ways. He always submitted His desire to the will of the Father. "Not My will, but Thine be done" was the practice of His life. His needs were always taken care of, but all of His desires were not.

A pastoral scene of green pastures and still waters follows in this psalm. Christ was provided for with both temporal and spiritual needs in daily rest, nourishment and grace. His life was one of peace and contentment in the midst of extreme temptation and suffering. In taking upon Himself the sin of the world He knows how hard it is for the transgressor, yet He also knew that the paths of righteousness were and are the ways of peace.

### "Thy rod and Thy staff."

In these symbols we have the assurance of protection, guidance, comfort, and discipline. The rod was used to protect the sheep from predators such as the bear and the lion. It was also used to discipline and to correct the sheep. The staff or crook was used to guide and to instruct as well as to correct. When a sheep needed to be pulled into line from going the wrong way or from going astray, the shepherd placed the staff around the neck of that sheep and gently pulled it back into the path. It was used to reach out to guide the sheep and urge it forward in the right direction.

With both the rod and the staff the sheep were protected and disciplined to obey, so that in times of danger and stress they would be safe under the guidance of the shepherd. The sheep were so disciplined that they would obey the voice of the shepherd in any time of trouble. So it was with Jesus. He was disciplined for Calvary from birth. It took discipline and obedience for Him to die. Jesus "learned obedience" from the things He suffered (Hebrews 5:8). He was obedient to death, "even the death of the cross" (Philippians 2:8).

Christ could not keep Himself alive; the devil could not keep Him dead. A dead Christ is stronger than a living devil! The devil could not keep Him in the grave. Christ died the equivalent of the death of the eternally damned. He died *for* us, *with* us, *as* us. And because Jesus went through that valley of death you may have assurance that He will never leave you nor forsake you in life or in death. Therefore you shall "fear no evil."

**"Thou preparest a table for Me in the presence of Mine enemies: thou anointest My head with oil; My cup runneth over" (verse 5).**

Here the shepherd-sheep imagery gives way to a banquet scene. Again provision and safety are pictured. More than survival after the walk through the valley of death is here. Triumph is revealed. He is the resurrection and the life.

Next come the oil and the overflowing cup. These awaited Christ's return to heaven after His ascension. In the Old Testament, eating and drinking at someone's table was a special time. It signified acceptance, respect and honor. At times it was a culminating symbol of a covenant. This was experienced by Moses, the priests and the seventy elders when they went up into the mount with God during the time Moses was given God's law which he taught the people (see Exodus 24:8-12; compare 1 Corinthians 11:25). So it was with Jesus when He went to heaven. Not only was He accepted, respected, and honored, He was worshipped by the angels.

The overflowing cup and the oil are symbols of an inauguration ceremony. After Christ was raised from the dead He remained on earth forty more days. Then ten days after Jesus went to heaven the Holy Spirit was sent, symbolized by fire, to the waiting disciples in the upper room in Jerusalem on the day of Pentecost. This was celebrated fifty days following the Passover (see Acts 1:3-2:1). Pentecost was the feast day that celebrated the giving of the law to Israel at Mt. Sinai.

But more than that, this particular Pentecost was heaven's announcement that Jesus had been inaugurated in heaven as man's High Priest and only Mediator. The ceremony was symbolized by anointing the high priest in the Jewish economy. Psalm 133:1, 2 presents to us the anointing of Aaron and what it signified: "Behold, how good and how pleasant it is for brethren to dwell together in unity! It is like the precious oil upon the head, running down on the beard, the beard of Aaron, running down on the edge of his garments."

The condition of unity that that psalm depicts was seen on the day of Pentecost as recorded in Acts 2:1-3: "They were all with one accord in one place ... Then there appeared to them divided tongues of fire, and one sat upon each of them. And they were all filled with the Holy Spirit." Both oil and fire symbolizes the activity of the Holy Spirit. Oil makes for smooth associations and relationships of working parts while fire indicates an all consuming desire to further God's gospel and work. Both oil and fire are needed in God's work on earth.

The ceremonies in heaven completed, the Holy Spirit was sent to Christ's waiting disciples. Their attention was directed to heaven and to Christ and His work in behalf of mankind. Their testimony ever after was of Christ raised from

the grave, of Christ ascended to heaven, and of Christ crucified (see Acts 2:22-36).

**"Surely goodness and mercy shall follow Me all the
days of My life: and I will dwell in the house of the Lord
for ever" (Psalm 23:6).**

The word translated "follow" means to pursue. What
was true of Christ is true of those who follow Him. God led
Him, followed Him, and pursued Him while He was a man on
the earth. His mercy surrounds Him today at the mercy seat
in Heaven.

And God's mercy surrounds you and me. It goes before
you and follows you. Enemies from within and from without
may (and do) pursue, but God and His mercy and grace are
much greater. He pursues you even more than all your enemies put together.

**Psalm 24 depicts Christ's ascension to the New Jerusalem
in heaven.**

He is accompanied by a choir of angels. Beginning with
verse 7 you may listen to the heavenly choir singing antipho-
nally. Part of the choir sings, followed by a brief silence, then
another part of the choir answers. This was the manner in
which the Jews approached Old Jerusalem feast days as they
traveled, singing the songs of Zion. As they neared Jerusalem
they sang this particular psalm, evidently the song angels
would sing as they escorted Christ back to heaven when they
came to the gates of the New Jerusalem.

Verse 7. "Lift up your heads, O you gates! And be lifted
up, you everlasting doors! And the King of glory shall come in,"
sang the entourage of angels as they approached the gates of
heaven.

Verse 8. "Who is this King of glory?" [Sang the awaiting
angels at the gates of heaven]. The escorting angels replied,
"The Lord strong and mighty, the Lord mighty in battle."

Verse 9. "Lift up your heads, O you gates! And lift them up, you everlasting doors! And the King of glory shall come in."

Verse 10. Again the question is asked, "Who is this King of glory?" And the reply, "The Lord of hosts, He is the King of glory."

These verses provide the background of Christ's ascension to heaven where He began His ministry in the heavenly sanctuary. This was preparation for the great enthronement and celebration that would be held after Christ entered the gates of the City. What rejoicing must have taken place at that time!

This may very well be a description of events that will occur again after the second Advent, when all the representatives of the universe travel to heaven to meet Christ and His glorified saints rescued from earth. Again the angels will break into rapturous singing. We will hear music we've never before heard, and our hearts will thrill through and through as we take part in the singing and as we listen to the thanksgiving and the glory and the praise given to the Father and to the Son.

# Chapter 3

## The Golgotha Psalm

## Psalm 22

Psalm 22 is one of, if not the best known, of the psalms about Jesus. Some students of Scripture have attempted to find a time and place where this psalm might be identified with David's experiences, but to no avail. What is described in this Psalm no one but Christ experienced. From beginning to end it is "Christ and Him crucified" only.

**It begins with the cry of anguish, "My God, My God, why have You forsaken Me?"**

This was the fourth "saying" of Christ on the cross, the first of His strong cries of agony as He was crushed to death by the torture of sin and guilt.

Even though He knew beforehand that this experience was going to take place, Jesus was surprised by the strangeness of it. Never before had He experienced anything like this. John Flavel in the seventeenth century observed that when Christ spoke these words, He did so in two languages. "Here is an observable variation of the language in which this astonishing complaint was uttered; for he speaks both Hebrew and Syriac in one breath. *Eli, Eli, lama,* are all Hebrew, *Sabachthani* is a Syriac word, used here for emphasis sake" (*The Works of John Flavel*, Vol. 1, p. 407).

Have you ever listened to a person who, knowing more than one language, when under extreme mental stress reverts back to the mother language? So it was with Jesus.

No doubt He knew several languages and dialects. Languages He would have been familiar with are Latin, Greek, Aramaic, and of course, Hebrew. Greek was the international language of that day, just as English is today. Jesus in mental anguish cried out both in Hebrew and Syriac (an ancient Aramaic language).

In this state of mind, Christ's memories recalled the sacred history of His people. "Our fathers trusted in You; they trusted and You delivered them. They cried to You, and were delivered; they trusted in You and were not ashamed" (Psalm 22;4, 5). He recalled the way that God had led them in the past. He next contrasted that history to His present circumstance.

**"But I am a worm, and no man, a reproach of men, and despised of the people. All those who see Me laugh Me to scorn; they shoot out the lip, they shake the head, saying He trusted in the Lord, let Him rescue him; Let Him deliver Him, since He delights in Him!" (verses 6-8).**

Resentment for the faith of Jesus is revealed in the words of those who crucified Him. Those words are the very ones uttered, perhaps unknowingly, the day of the crucifixion. The fulfillment of this part of the psalm is recorded in Matthew 27:39-43.

In the psalm under consideration, beginning with verse 9, we read of Christ's personal history as He was protected by the Father from the time of His birth into the human family. "But You are He who took Me out of the womb; You made Me trust when I was on My mother's breasts." The margin of the King James Version puts it this way: You "kept Me in safety."

There were many attempts on the life of Jesus. This began shortly after His birth by the puppet king, Herod. But God kept Him in safety until the fullness of the time came for Him to endure the full weight of the sins of the world. That time now came. "I was cast upon You from birth. From My mother's womb, You have been My God. Be not far from Me, for trouble is near; for there is none to help" (verses 10, 11).

Humans and devils are next portrayed as wild raging, ravenous beasts who lusted to tear Him limb from limb as seen in their inhuman treatment of the Innocent One (verses 12, 13, 16, 20, 21).

Next comes a word picture of His physical and emotional sufferings as He hung upon the cross. He went limp from the tortuous condition He was in. His bones at the joints began to separate. His mind melted like wax in fire. His strength drained from Him like liquid from a broken vessel. His tongue swelled and stuck to His jaws. Inflammation of wounds, high temperature, thirst and mental anguish are all there in the prophecy of verses 14, 15.

Christ's bones stuck out, hanging exposed in His nakedness on the cross, as soldiers gambled over His garments strewn on the ground before Him (verse 18). His certain death was assumed by those religious and non–religious wretches that day on Mount Calvary.

But they were surprised that it came so soon. They were going to help the death process, those merchants of death. However, when they went to break His legs to hasten the expiration, they found He was dead already! And so the prophecy was fulfilled in that although His hands and feet were pierced by the spikes, His bones were not broken (verse 17).

Just before Jesus died He prayed a prayer of anguish and triumph. He asked for God's presence, for help, for deliverance. And He was heard. He said, "You have answered Me" (verse 21). His deliverance came in death.

The remainder of the chapter is a song of the triumph of faith. These were the things passing rapidly through His mind in the closing minutes of His life. Victory is promised here for those who will not turn away from so costly and so great a salvation.

That sacrifice for our redemption was accomplished in Christ. One of the last words of Christ on the cross was, "It is finished" (John 19:30). And the last word in the original of Psalm 22 is, "finished."

**This word is rich in meaning.**

The word "finished" is a primitive root word that means "to do" or "to make" as in creation (Genesis 1:7; 2:2-4), "to accomplish" (Isaiah 55:11), or "to finish." It is used in connection with the offerings in the ceremonial system: "sacrifice" (Leviticus 23:19); "offering" (9:2, 7, 16, 22; 16:9); the morning and evening sin offering (Exodus 29:38); and for making incense (30:34-38).

Both the offerings and the incense, ascending with the prayers of Israel represent the merits of Christ's righteousness and intercession. During His life and in death He earned the right to represent mankind in the courts of heaven. His merits, through faith, are imputed to His believing people, and these merits make the worship of sinful beings acceptable to God (Ephesians 5:1. 2; 1:6). Christ finished the work on earth He had been sent to do. In Psalm 22:31 the word "finished" implies the carrying through of the work of redemption by God in Christ, on the cross. It is echoed by those who proclaim His righteousness. And in Isaiah 44:23 we find a call to inanimate nature to rejoice in what God accomplished—our redemption.

And now in the sanctuary in heaven Christ works as the only Mediator between God and man. He is there finishing the work of redemption that He began while on earth.

# Chapter 4

## The State of His Mind

## Psalm 22:1, 14

Our topic for this chapter is again from Psalm 22. We will consider two verses 1 and 14, as one. Christ on the cross cried out in forsakenness. In that terrible state of mind, He quoted Psalm 22:1: "My God, my God, why have You forsaken Me? Why are You so far from helping Me, and from the words of My groaning?"—or as the King James Version puts it, "from my roaring?"

The word roaring comes from a root word that means to howl in pain like a beast. Christ, in mental anguish screamed in pain, sounding more like the agonizing cry of a wild beast in pain than a human being. The cacophonous screams of His voice echoed the state of His mind as He felt the breakup of His union with His heavenly Father. This was the only time from eternity that such a separation took place within the Godhead.

As much as we can understand of it, let's consider Christ's mental anguish. But when we are through here, there will be much more to it than we can possibly understand.

**Verse 14: "I'm poured out like water, and all my bones are out of joint: my heart is like wax; it has melted within me."**

Strong muscles became like liquid through the torturous ordeal He went through. The physical coming apart at the joints was a faint reflection of His mental state as He felt the full force and load of the sin of us all as it was laid upon Him. His heart became like wax under the heat of fire. The heart in Hebrew thought means the intellect as well as the emotions. His mind was going through the process of a meltdown from the crushing pressure of grief, just as wax changes to a liquid state by the application of heat.

Sin burns like a fire in the mind (Isaiah 8:18). It melts and consumes the nervous system. Anyone unprotected from its raging fierceness is destroyed.

The word "melt" means to be dissolved by fear or terror, or by the wasting of disease. It is applied also to fainting that comes from fear, grief, or sorrow. As used here it describes the disorientation of Christ's mind as He felt the guilt and shame of our sins within His nervous system. The pent up fires of hell burst upon Him at Calvary with all the fury of atomic energy. Sin was consuming Jesus. This was equivalent to the experience of the lake of fire about which the Revelator writes (Revelation 20).

This experience was the previously anticipated hour that caused Him to tremble. Recorded in John 12 when the Gentiles came to see Him in the temple court, He knew their coming was a fulfillment of prophecy. He knew that their coming to Him would be one of the evidences that He was on target with His mission to redeem mankind. He cried out, "God, save Me from this hour." There was a fierce struggle within, between His emotions and His determination to do God's will. Then He said in submission, "But for this came I into this hour. Father glorify Me." The cross was the glorification of Christ.

**What we observe in this psalm and others is the meltdown of the mind of Christ.**

It was melting like wax as He was made to be sin for us. Sin worked its defeating and disheartening effect upon

His mind. Convulsions of agony racked His mind as well as His frame. Agony suggests mental or physical torment so excruciating that body and/or mind are convulsed from the force of it. The horrors of the curse were upon Him. Feelings of guilt and condemnation tortured Him. This is a horrible sight. But its awfulness is our salvation.

Although He knew no sin, He was *made to be sin* for us. He did not sin, but sin destroyed Him. Our sin, guilt, and condemnation were imputed to Him. This was just as certain and real to Him as it is when His righteousness is imputed to us. He was conscious of imputed sins to Himself. He felt the weight of them. They devastated and demolished Him. There were disturbances in His mind and in His feelings. But even through this meltdown, the faith of Jesus held. The beginning verse of Psalm 22 presents the faith and the feelings of Jesus. "My God! My God!" Those words express the faith of Jesus. Then His feelings spoke: "Why have You forsaken Me?" Faith spoke first and it spoke twice.

There are two aspects of faith. Belief is one of them. This is not necessarily saving faith. Devils believe, they tremble. But it doesn't save them. Appreciation is another aspect of faith. There are times when we feel good. We have joy. This comes from appreciating what God has done for us and for His goodness toward us when we know we deserve it not. But even this is not saving faith. Saving faith is the faith of Jesus. This is the faith that not only believes in the absence of feelings, but against them. In the last days of earth's history, God's people will receive the full cup of Christ's faith (Revelation 14:12). It comes through the message of Christ crucified and His righteousness. Christ on Calvary came to the end of His rope. But His faith held.

There were disturbances in the thoughts and in the feelings of Jesus, but not in His attitude or in His faith. Never before had He undergone anything like this. He sinned not. He was sinless in His choices and in His thinking, though powerfully pulled to yield. The devil was trying to break Him down so that He might sin. While it is true that He experienced despair, despondency and discouragement, He did not descend to the level of personal sin in these feelings. There are some today who believe these feelings are sins. But this is not so in all cases. They can *become* sin. Despondency and despair can come because of selfishness, but not always. There are times when these negative feelings come from a physical weakness.

**Chemical or hormonal imbalances can likewise upset our mental state.**

These are not to be classed as sin. Some persons love to feel depressed or despondent. Some love to feel sorry for themselves. This *is* sin. But feelings of despondency and despair are not sins in and of themselves. Jesus felt the full force of despair and never sinned. He knows by experience what we from time to time go through. He also knows how much grace we need in those terrible times, for He is touched with the feelings of our infirmities and He knows how to bring to us help in those times of temptation.

In Christ's experience, it was human sin that caused the intense burning suffering within His emotional and mental faculties. Although He felt as though God had forever forsaken Him, His faith held fast to the throne of God's grace. He refused to be denied. His faith was His anchor during this storm. It took thirty-three years of submission to His Father's will, thirty-three years of temptation and trial, to prepare Christ for this time of supreme testing.

He could not have withstood this trial as a child. As a child He had the experiences of a child. He grew as a child, He spoke as a child. He developed as a child. He had the faith of a child. When He grew to manhood He put away the ways of His childhood. But the character developed by faith that always obeyed in His childhood—that was foundational to all the temptations of His life, especially the last temptation. The faith of the little child developed continually to the point of His death. Christ's entire life was one of faith. He learned by faith; He was sanctified by faith, He walked by faith; in short, He lived by faith. There was only one thing He did not do by faith and that was to die, but He died *in* faith that His Father would resurrect Him from the grave.

Christ was tempted by the devil in the wilderness shortly after He was baptized. The words of the Heavenly Father , "This is My Beloved Son in whom I am pleased," were ringing in the devil's mind. Those words of affirmation were the first audible words from the Father to Christ, and thus to the human race since sin entered the human race. In those words God spoke to the human race, fallen as it was and yet is. The pronouncement was that "He has made us accepted in the Beloved" (Ephesians 1:6). Christ became the Public Man, the Representative Man, the last Adam. Christ as the Head of the race met and defeated the human foe in the wilderness temptations. Faith in the word of God was the first public test.

The devil first tempted the Representative Man, Christ Jesus, on the point of appetite just as he did the first Adam. He tried to get Christ to act as God in creating food to save Himself. Jesus replied as the Public Man: "It is written that man shall not live by bread only, but by every word that proceeds out of the mouth of God" (Matthew 4:4). This "it is written" comes from Deuteronomy 8:3 that says literally, in the original language, "*adam* shall not live by bread alone, but by every word coming out of the mouth of God." This means living by faith. Christ, by faith in God's word, on behalf of the human race, defeated the devil in the wilderness. But this was not His supreme test.

In Gethsemane and on the cross, Jesus again met this temptation in all the fullness of its force. Bearing the full weight of the sins of the world, in the weakness of human nature, and weakened to the point of exhaustion, Christ was again tempted to use creative energy to escape from the pit of despair and despondency in Gethsemane, and from destruction on Calvary.

Although Christ was tempted at every step of His human life, beginning with Gethsemane was the hour of "the power of darkness" which Jesus dreaded to enter. But He knew He must. This was the final testing hour, the last hour for the last Adam, for the last time. And it was the last time for the devil also. It was now all or nothing. The stakes were high for both warriors.

These two who in another world at another time were the closest of friends now were enemies. Lucifer because of insubordination was dismissed from his position and place in heaven. Now he had the advantage. Christ, his commander in heaven, who became part of His own creation to save that part of His creation, was much weaker in physical strength and in mental ability as a man. Could Christ, the Son of Man, withstand the onslaught that awaited His mind for the next 18 hours?

Their time had fully come. Christ would be given completely into the hands of the devil, to find if the devil could shake Christ from His faith. That shaking time proved decisively the superiority of the Word of God and the faith of Jesus, weak as He was as a man. God demonstrated that with all the weaknesses of the flesh, with all the committed sins of the world heaped upon Christ, God's grace is stronger than all the power of the Devil.

## But God, the Father, must have trembled in that fearful hour.

All heaven was risked at Calvary. Had Christ failed (and that was a real possibility!) more than the human race would have been involved. There were cosmic proportions of which we know nothing. We can only get hints of them from the inspired word. These will have to wait until the second coming of Christ when He shall explain all things.

## Psalm 18 reveals David's ordeal with his enemies and his deliverance.

This typifies Christ and His death. In verse 4 we learn of fear on the part of Christ because of the onslaughts of the Devil. Waves of sin and death engulfed Christ. This made Him experience fear as no one else has. To repeat, *there is a fear that is not unto sin.* The feelings of fear may seem to overwhelm us. But as David wrote in another place, "Whenever I am afraid, I will trust in You" (Psalm 56:3). Even in times of heartbreaking, abject fear, the faith of Jesus will hold us fast in God's care.

This psalm is a promise— one that no doubt blessed Christ. It is a promise for you and for me today also. The Devil will at times terrify you. He may awaken you from sleep in the night. There may be a heaviness that can be felt in your room. You may experience difficulty in breathing. You may not be able to utter a sound from your lips. But in your mind you can still pray, "Jesus save me, Jesus help me." He understands. He will deliver. When afraid, you can trust God.

Psalm 18: 5. "Then the sorrows of Sheol (hell) surrounded me; the snares of death confronted me." That place, that hell, that death, is not the grave to which all our feet are directed. That is the place of separation, equivalent to the second death at the end of the thousand years recorded in Revelation 20. Christ paid that penalty. The penalty is not the first, but the second death, our wages for our sin. The first death is called a sleep by Jesus (John 11:11-14). The first death is a consequence of sin and not a punishment in the most strict sense of the meaning. In the superhuman agony into which Christ was plunged, it is written, "In my distress I called upon the Lord, and cried out to My God; He heard My voice from His temple, and My cry came before Him, even to His ears" (Psalm 18:6).

In the following verses we see the reaction of nature as the footsteps of God approach Calvary:

"Then the earth shook and trembled; the foundations of the hills quaked and were shaken, because He was angry. Smoke went up from His nostrils, and devouring fire from His mouth; coals were kindled by it. He bowed the heavens also, and came down with darkness under His feet. And He rode upon the cherub, and flew; He flew upon the wings of the wind. He made darkness His secret place; His canopy around Him was dark waters and thick clouds of the skies" (Psalm 18:7-11).

As sin worked its destructive way through the nervous system of Christ, while the devil was manifesting the malignity of his hatred against Christ, God came from heaven to be by the side of His beloved Son. Although there was a violent severance between the Persons of the Godhead because of sin, yet the Father came as close to Jesus as He could. He could not remain in heaven. He longed to bring Christ some assurance and hope as He was being put to death, but He could not. He could look on in horror, but He could not help the Man who was His fellow Companion from eternal ages.

In your mind's eye, picture the Father standing next to His suffering Son, trembling and weeping, longing to comfort Him. God put His own Omnipotence under restraint as He refrained from breaking through the darkness to deliver His agonizing Son. The sufferings of the cross give a glimpse into the agony that exists in the heart of God because of sin. That agony did not end, neither did it begin there.

As Christ died, the Father could not speak of what was then transpiring. The heavenly angels were silent, for they did not know all there was to know about what was happening to the mind of Christ. Christ's disciples were in total darkness. Their minds were as dark as the day turned night, as the sun refused to shine. In the silence of any spoken word, inanimate nature cried out and preached the gospel. Nature spoke with a clear loud voice.

The testimony of Jesus was revealed in the hiding of the sun's rays that day. As with the day, His mind was covered with a pall of darkness, darker than midnight pitch. No hope presented itself to the mind of Jesus as the full weight of sin settled down upon His mind and spirit. Christ committed no sin, but He felt as though He committed all the sins of the world. He was made to be sin itself in order for us, in Him, to be made the righteousness of God (2 Corinthians 5:21).

The darkened heavens speak of a deeper gloom that engulfed the mind of Jesus:

- Absence of light from His Father,
- Dismay,
- Dejection,
- Despair,
- Hopelessness,
- Depression,
- Despondency,
- Inexpressible sorrow and grief.

Finally, with nervous exhaustion came the loss of hope and a sense of futility. He was gripped with a paralyzing fear. Filled with emotions of anxiety and dread, He experienced within Himself intense and prolonged feelings of insecurity. Troubled by alienation from God, guilt and excessive grief racked His mind.

**But there was more to come.**

The end was not yet. Not by themselves did those tenebrous hours reveal the state of Christ's mind as He died. The earth likewise preached the gospel of Christ crucified. Just as the earthquake tore boulders from the earth and flung them out, so it was that sin ripped through the mind of Jesus Christ and caused a greater earthquake within His very being.

The condition of Christ's mind at that very time was preached by rent rocks. Those rocks torn from the firm foundations within earth's crust by the upheaval of the underlying activities of intense heat and shifting earth masses, revealed the state of Christ's mind melting from the fierce heat and pressure of sin realized by Him when He screamed, "My God, My God, why have You forsaken Me!" Here we get the picture of mental breakdown under the hammering force of sin.

Christ's body and mind went into convulsions that He could not control. Jesus was in a greater mental and emotional earthquake than the convulsions that tore the rocks from the earth. The rent rocks cried out at the violent disturbances ripping through Christ's mind as it was pulled apart by sin on Calvary. Christ was taken to the edge of insanity and total mental breakdown. But He did not break. His faith held to the reality of God's word. Be amazed and wonder! He was made to be sin itself. And all this for you.

During all of this, God stood by the cross next to His Son. God stood there in the mantle of darkness. That mantle was His "pavilion" by which He drew near to His Son and consequently to the entire human race. As Christ cried out in agony, the Father unseen, trembling, unheard, wept and whispered, Here I am, here I am. I have heard Your cry, but this is the only way; this is the plan You laid out in heaven.

Deity suffered. Deity sank at Calvary. God suffered with His Son. He suffered in silence as He felt Their oneness breaking up. Then at the time of the evening sacrifice, the Son yielded up His life while addressing the Father, "It is finished." "Into Thy hands I commend My spirit" (John 19:30; Luke 23:46, KJV). When Jesus was driven to the edge of insanity, when He got to the end of His rope of faith, it held! It maintained control over His mind during His time of trouble that was more severe in intensity than Jacob's. The faith of Jesus conquered. God, the Father, triumphed with Him.

And God caused light to shine out of the darkness of the mind of His dear Son, on Calvary to redeem us (2 Corinthians 4:6).

# The Two Adams
# Psalm 8

Psalm 8 is a prophecy which foretold that Christ would bless the children and that He would be proclaimed King by children. The psalm begins, "O Lord, our Lord, how excellent is Your name in all the earth, You who set Your glory above the heavens! Out of the mouth of babes and infants You have ordained strength, because of Your enemies, that You may silence the enemy and the avenger."

This passage was connected with the cleansing of the temple by Jesus as recorded in Matthew 12:12-16. The temple courts had been made into a center for trading commodities. The people were terrified when Jesus came into the temple complex and rattled the moneychangers. They fled, but the children remained. The children were not afraid of Jesus. Business as usual was interrupted and the exchangers fled in fear, but the children sang praises to the Lord.

The people who fled chagrined and angry returned to the temple courts and heard the children singing. They tried to get Jesus to silence them. Christ quoted the psalm under consideration, "Out of the mouths of babes You have perfected praise" to show the people that this was a fulfillment of prophecy (see Matthew 21:16). Christ asserted His rightful place as the second Adam as the psalm reveals.

The psalm continues. "What is man that You are mindful of him, and the son of man that You visit him? For You have made him a little lower than the angels, and You have crowned him with glory and honor. You have made him to have dominion over the works of Your hands; You have put all things under His feet ..." (verses 4-6). This was quoted by Paul in 1 Corinthians 15:27 when he referred to the second coming of Christ. All things will be turned over to Him at the second Advent, at the resurrection of the body of believers.

Verses 4 and 5 are quoted in Hebrews 2:6-8 to apply to Christ. In the beginning this applied to Adam, but because Christ is the second and last Adam, it applies to Him also. Hebrews 2:9: "But we see Jesus, who was made a little lower than the angels, for the suffering of death crowned with glory and honor, that He, by the grace of God might taste death for everyone." Paul quotes Psalm 8, then applies it to Christ. The first Adam was made a little lower than the angels, and the second Adam likewise was made a little lower than the angels.

But it was "for the suffering of death" that Christ was made to be mortal. As God He could not die. Even if He had come like Adam was in his pre-fall nature, Christ could not have died. But He was *made* to die, He was *born* to die. He was made to taste death for everyone, by the grace of God. That He was made mortal was imperative.

While man is described in this psalm as powerless and frail, he is not forgotten by God. God looks after and cares for him.

Psalm 8 ends as it begins with identical words, praising the Lord. This is called an envelope construction. Contained within these praises we learn of God's purpose in man's creation. This psalm is a lyric echo of Moses' account of creation. God's glory is observed in the realm of nature and in the realm of Providence, and through these to its contemplation in the kingdom of grace.

The chapter outlined as an envelope chiasm appears like this:

A. God's sovereignty—vs . 1
B. God's dominion—vss. 2, 3
C. Man's insignificance—vs. 4
C. Man's exaltation—vs. 5
B. Man's dominion—vss. 6–8
A. God's sovereignty—vs. 9.

To Adam, who was made "a little lower than the angels" was given dominion over God's creation (verses 5 and 6). The first Adam surrendered himself and his dominion to the enemy of God. Because of that, this psalm can be fulfilled only in Christ, and by Him as the second Adam.

As mentioned above, Jesus quoted verse two of this psalm when His dominion over the temple was questioned. Five days before He died, Christ cleansed the temple again and restored it to its proper use for a short period of time. Rather than being used as a market place for the world's trade and rather than a den for the religious establishment to hide their thievery, it was to be "a house of prayer for all people" (Isaiah 56:7). Christ transformed it into a place of ministry for the physically disabled and for sin-sick souls (Matthew 21:12-14).

After being driven from the temple courts, "the chief priests and scribes" sneaked back in. They saw the blind and the lame going to Jesus to be healed. They heard praises to Christ from the children, and they were enraged because of the children's hosannas. Their consciences seared from resistance to the Holy Spirit, these pretenders could not recognize the fulfillment in Christ as the second Adam of Psalm 8. And so they demanded of Him, "Do You hear what these are saying?" "Yes," Jesus replied, then directed the attention of those charlatans to Psalm 8:2, "Have you never read, 'Out of the mouth of babes and nursing infants You have perfected praise'?" (Matthew 21:16).

God chooses the weak and foolish things to confound the mighty men of earth. God works most effectively through the things and the persons despised by the wise of the earth. The mysteries of God are revealed to children, but hidden from the wise and intelligent of the world (1 Corinthians 1:27-29; Acts 4:13; 6:8, 10).

Those doubters could not see that God was mindful of them, and that He cared for and visited man in fulfillment of Psalm 8. What was hidden from those earthly wise men because of their unbelief was revealed to believing children. But the experience of the children could not penetrate the heart of those religious leaders. And so as Christ left the temple that Sunday evening, their day of grace ended.

In the light of the New Testament, Psalm 8 is a prophecy of Christ the second Adam and of the new humanity as redeemed by Him. The central thought of the psalm is restated, then continued. It reveals the loss of dominion by Adam, then its restoration through Christ. Hebrews 2:6-8 reveals the sovereign dominion of Christ by showing that He is the Man God has crowned with glory and honor and made to have dominion over all the works of creation.

In typical Hebrew fashion, David used synonymous parallelism to describe the last Adam and God's care for Him:

"What is man [*enosh*] that You mindful of him,

"And the son of man [*ben* adam] that You care for him?" (Psalm 8:4, margin).

Both Hebrew words *enosh'* and *adam* are terms describing a representative man who is the head of the race. Both words are used rarely in the sense of a single individual. They are usually used in a collective or corporate sense such as the entire human race. In this psalm they are used to describe especially Christ in His representative function for the race. The word *enosh'* is never used of man before the fall. It is used to describe man's fallen and thus mortal condition according to his nature which is inherited. It is "used of the Messiah, Psalm 8:4." "This ... passage applies to Christ *solely;* see Heb. 2:6" (*Gesenius's Hebrew and Chaldee Lexicon,* p. 63, emphasis original. See also *Wilson's Old Testament Word Studies,* p. 266).

The Aramaic cognate *enash'* is used of Christ in Daniel 7:13. Here we view Christ as the Elder Brother of the race representing us before the throne of God in scenes of the judgment. He receives the dominion and the kingdom in behalf of His people. Judgment is given in behalf of those He represents (see verses 14, 18, 22).

The use of the term *enosh'* indicates Christ's real affinity with the fallen human race. He became one of us in order to be "touched with the feelings of our infirmities" (Hebrews 4:15). This is not the modern idea of the cosmological and pantheistic "christ" worshipped by spiritual Babylon under the New Age scheme of things.

The true Christ felt a real identity with man. The Son of Man became the Savior of the world (John 4:42; 1 Timothy 4:10). In order to become man it was essential that He become part of the race in the deepest and fullest sense. He took upon Himself our fallen nature in order to redeem the human race. At conception He took our nature and entered into man's alienation from God, even though He was never guilty of actual sin. He never allowed His inherited nature to rebel against the will of God. He came not to do His will, but the will of the Father (John 5:30).

The greatest honor bestowed upon the human race is in the fact that the Son of God took upon Himself our nature in the incarnation, and then lived by faith according to God's will in our behalf. And being a man, God visited and cared for Him, and thus visits and cares for you.

Hebrews 2 takes up Psalm 8 and, applying it to Christ, lays the foundation for the presentation of the humanity of Christ in the book of Hebrews. After quoting Psalm 8:4-6, Paul writes: "For in that He put all in subjection under Him, He left nothing that is not put under Him. But now we do not yet see all things put under Him" (Hebrews 2:6-8). Something happened to Adam's dominion. He sinned, and now because he lost control of himself, he could not control his dominion. But "we see" Someone else!

"But we see Jesus, who was made a little lower than the angels, for the suffering of death crowned with glory and honor ..." (verse 9). He met Adam at his lowest point—death. This was a lower state than where Adam was when he was first created. It was impossible for Adam to die before he sinned. And so, we can see that Christ came not to the place where Adam was *before* he fell, "but we see Jesus for the suffering *of death*." This was much lower than where Adam began. In order for Christ to die He had to become mortal. Mortality came into existence because of sin. As soon as one is conceived, he inherits the propensity to die. The seeds of death are in *fallen* human nature. In order for Christ to enter the "suffering of death" He had to be "made of a woman" with a mortal nature.

## As God, Christ was immortal.

But He laid aside this attribute and took upon Himself mortality in order to be "numbered with the transgressors" and to die in our stead. He was "made ... for the suffering of death ... that He by the grace of God might taste death for everyone." Unfallen angels know nothing of grace personally. They are not under grace, having never sinned. Adam before he fell did not need grace. Grace came in because of sin. Christ was made to be sin for us. Christ needed grace. And it was by the grace of God that He tasted eternal death for the fallen race. It was by grace, God's enabling grace, that Christ tasted death for every human. This grace is the same as that given to every human since the fall of Adam. This grace is given only to those born into this world, born in sinful fallen human nature. Christ was not exempt from grace. He needed it from Bethlehem to Calvary. He lived and grew in grace. And by grace He tasted death for us all (John 1:14; Luke 2:40; Hebrews 2:9).

Christ could not have died if He had taken the unfallen nature of angels or the sinless nature of pre-fall Adam. Can you imagine how the angels of heaven became grief-stricken when they learned that Christ would assume man's mortal nature? He, who as God, was superior to them, would become inferior to them when He should assume human nature. He who created them would be in need of their wisdom and strength and comfort.

When Adam sinned against known light, the entire race that was to come from him was doomed to condemnation and everlasting destruction. But God had a plan. He was not caught off-guard. He made Himself responsible for man's failure. He became Surety for man. This is why "we see Jesus, who was made a little lower than the angels, for the suffering of death. ..." He became "the Lamb slain from the foundation of the world" (Revelation 13:8). In the beginning, the altar of sacrifice and the promise of redemption were placed side by side, each casting light on the other (Genesis 4:3, 4; 3:15).

The first promise of redemption for man is addressed to "that serpent of old, the Devil and Satan": "I will put enmity between you and the woman, and between your seed and her Seed," God declared. "He will bruise your head, and you will bruise His heel" (Revelation 12:9; Genesis 3:15). Satan was made to realize that he was not to have free reign over his usurped dominion taken from mankind. God promised to enter more directly into the battle for man. He promised nothing but enmity between the Seed of the woman and the followers of Satan.

When the full force of the promise dawned upon the devil's mind, he found cause for rejoicing. In order for him to bruise the heel of the promised Seed of the woman, her Seed would have to be made vulnerable. He had to be made touchable and bruisable. The devil could not do this unless Christ should be "made a little lower than the angels, for the suffering of death." He rejoiced that he could pull down the Son of God from the throne of the universe to the level of fallen man. With Christ in human nature the devil was confident that He could cause Christ to sin. From the time of the promise of Genesis 3:15 forward, the enemy planned and experimented on fallen human nature. He wanted both to weaken human nature, in order to place Christ at a great disadvantage when

He became human, and to experiment to find the easiest access to the fallen nature of man.

**Christ was not only bruised by Satan.**

He was bruised also by mankind's sins. "All we like sheep have gone astray, we have turned, every one, to his own way; and the Lord has laid on Him the iniquity of us all." "And by His stripes we are healed" (Isaiah 53:6, 5). Christ was "made a little lower than the angels for the suffering of death" (Hebrews 2:9).

He was made for death! This death was not the first death that everyone dies. The first death is a consequence of Adam's sin, not the punishment for it. Jesus died the equivalent of the second death. He tasted "death for everyone" (Hebrews 2:9). Christ is the only one who has tasted the second death. No human being was intended, by God to die the second death. That death is a prepared death, only "prepared for the devil and his angels" (Matthew 25: 41). Humans who spurn and reject "the grace of God that brings salvation" that "has appeared to all men" will go with the devil into the lake of fire (Titus 2:11; Matthew 25:41).

**Christ by the grace of God tasted that death for all mankind.**

The fire of envy and hatred consumed Him. He tasted that death, beginning in Gethsemane. Had not heaven intervened, Christ would have perished there. There would have been no public execution on Calvary. Because it was a public death, a crucified Christ has been proclaimed in the world, to the world, and for all the world.

In bruising Christ by temptation and finally in death, the devil himself received a wound that cannot heal. By partaking of our same flesh and blood Christ was made to die, "that through death He might destroy him who had the power of death, that is, the devil" (Hebrews 2:14).

In another letter Paul in dealing with a misunderstanding and denial of the resurrection in the church of Corinth, quoted Psalm 8:6 in the context of the two Adams. What the first Adam did to us, Christ undid. "He has put all things under His feet." "For since by man came death, by Man also came the resurrection of the dead. For as in Adam all die, even so in Christ all shall be made alive" (1 Corinthians 15:27, 21, 22).

In his second letter to the Corinthian church Paul again took up the theme of the second Adam. "For the love of Christ constrains us, because we judge thus: that if One died for all, then all died" (2 Corinthians 5:14). In Christ, the Representative Man, the Head of mankind, the whole fallen human race died. Christ died not for Himself, but for you. He exhausted the penalty which was yours, that you might become the righteousness of God in Him (verse 21).

Although Adam carved his initials deep in our flesh, Christ carved His much deeper. What Adam did against us, Christ reversed. Christ's work for us is far greater than what Adam did to us.

The greatest honor bestowed upon the human race is in the fact that Christ took upon Himself our nature in the incarnation. And being a man, God visited Him, cared for Him and thus visits and cares for us. And the fact that Christ in glorified human nature sits at the side of the Father, God blesses us in Him (Ephesians 1:3,6). And so it is that Psalm 8, prophetic of Christ, was fulfilled in and by Christ.

This psalm will meet its complete fulfillment in the new earth. Verse 6: "You have put all things under His feet" will then be accomplished as it is written:

> "For since by man came death, by Man also came the resurrection of the dead. For as in Adam all die, even so in Christ all shall be made alive. But each one in his own order: Christ the firstfruits, afterward those who are Christ's at His coming. Then comes the end, when He delivers the kingdom to God the Father, when He puts an end to all authority and power. For

He must reign till He has put all enemies under
His feet. The last enemy that will be destroyed is
death. For 'He has put all things under His feet'"
(1 Corinthians 15:21-27).

Psalm 8 ends as it began—singing praises to God: "O
Lord, our Lord, How excellent is Your name in all the earth."

# Chapter 6

## Psalms About Jesus and Judas

## Psalms 41:9; 55:12-14

Jesus experienced feelings of pity and concern for Judas when He first saw him. As ambitious Judas pressed his way into the presence of Jesus, instantly He knew this was the man who would one day betray Him. Jesus read him like an open book. To outward appearances this stately looking person had all the qualifications for political success in the coming kingdom. But Jesus in the book of Psalms read about his true heart sentiments.

Judas became a leader and the treasurer of the little band of Christ's disciples. Contrary to appearances, Judas was merciless. The poor were not helped by him, except to further his own interests. He despised the very people Christ blessed—the broken in heart and the heavy laden.

The canker of covetousness was detected by Christ from the first. "Foxes have holes and birds have nests," Jesus said, "but the Son of man has nowhere to lay His head." From the psalms Jesus learned the character of His betrayer. He knew he would be a close ally, an associate.

Psalm 109, especially verses 6-20, outlines the character and consequential destiny, not only of Judas but also of his posterity. Verse 8 was quoted by Peter to the believers when Matthias was chosen to take Judas' place among the eleven apostles. "Let another take his office" (Acts 1:20). Three times the psalms concerning Judas are referred to in Acts 1. Along with Psalm 109:8, Psalm 69:25 is also quoted: "Let his habitation be desolate, and let no one live in it."

Peter said earlier:

"Men and brethren, this Scripture had to be fulfilled which the Holy Spirit spoke before by the mouth of David concerning Judas, who became a guide to those who arrested Jesus: for he was numbered with us and obtained a part in this ministry" (Acts 1:16,17).

This was in reference to Psalm 41:9 that prophesied of Judas' treatment of Jesus. "Even My own familiar friend in whom I trusted, who ate My bread, has lifted his heal against Me." Remember, this betrayal was not by an enemy, not by a stranger, but by a close friend. Hardest to bear is the reproach and betrayal of a friend! The thought is captured in Psalm 55:12-14:

"For it is not an enemy who reproaches me; then I could bear it. Nor is it one who hates me who has magnified himself against me; then I could hide from him. But it was you, a man my equal, my companion and my acquaintance. We took sweet counsel together, and walked to the house of God in the throng."

When Judas led the multitude of rabble to the place of prayer in the garden of Gethsemane, and there betrayed Jesus to them by that infamous kiss, Jesus asked "Friend, why have you come?" (Matthew 26:50). That question was unanswered, but you can be sure it never left Judas' mind until he died.

In return for Christ's unconditional love, Judas became His accuser. The destiny of Judas written in advance is found in Psalm 109: 6-15, the judgment of Judas and his descendants is there depicted. He opposed the mercy and grace of God as manifested in the life and actions of Jesus. The children of Judas, following his example, likewise opposed the grace of God that brings salvation to every person (Titus 2:11). The Psalmist predicted the misery and the destruction of Judas, the ringleader motivated by malice and revenge. No one, not even Jesus, escaped the malevolence of this deceptive "son of perdition."

It was Satan who influenced Judas against the Savior. Satan stood "at his right hand," suggesting to that keen mind of Judas thoughts which the fallen angel himself harbored ever since the days of his rebellion in heaven. Satan worked out through Judas his own feelings of revenge against Christ.

Like Judas, Lucifer at one time was drawn to the Son of God. Like Judas, he nursed feelings against Christ. Like Judas, he deceived some of Christ's closest friends. And like Judas on earth, Lucifer accused and betrayed Christ when they were friends together in heaven.

And in Christ's treatment of Judas we can understand how He dealt with Lucifer in heaven. On the evening of the last supper (for Judas as well as Christ) Jesus knelt before Judas to wash his feet. The Spirit of God in union with Jesus impressed powerfully the heart of Judas, drawing him to repent and return to God. Jesus there revealed to Judas and to the observing universe, the principle of leadership He employed in heaven, which is service. Christ, Master of all, is Servant of all. Judas and Lucifer before him perceived and understood the lesson. Both rejected this aspect of the character of God. Both accused Christ of rulership that was unacceptable to themselves. To cover themselves they accused Christ of their own selfishness. An accuser usually denounces another of the very thing which he desires and of which he is guilty.

By specific actions, Lucifer in heaven and Judas on earth disqualified themselves for companionship with Christ or with heaven. Each case was one of apostasy rather than of hypocrisy. Even so, Christ loved them. In the context of Lucifer's defection in heaven, Ezekiel wrote of Christ's lamentation for him in Ezekiel 28:12-19.

Read it from God's point of reference—with a broken heart. A lamentation is a deep grief, mourning and sorrow, as one hurts when a loved one dies. When Lucifer left Him, God wept. So it was with Jesus and Judas. Judas, His friend, sent arrows of agony into the heart of Christ as He reached out to him with *agape* love that was resisted and beaten back time after time. He would not *let* Christ save him.

Jesus did not refuse to ordain Judas to the gospel ministry, nor refuse him the power to work miracles, to cast out demons, and to heal the sick. Neither did He refuse the traitor's kiss of betrayal.

Judas' love of money and of the world overbalanced his love for Jesus. From time to time he responded partially to Christ's constraining love. But he would not fully surrender to its sovereignty. Avarice finally became the ruling motive in his life.

Judas opened his heart to unbelief. "The god of this world" blinded his mind "lest the light of the gospel of the glory of Christ ... should shine on" him (2 Corinthians 4:4, 5). Blindness came, not because he had no chance to believe, but rather because he closed his eyes to believing. Then he went blind, spiritually.

The turning point for Judas came about one year before he betrayed Jesus. At that time he probably did not know to what extent he would go. Jesus declared to His disciples then that one of them was governed by the devil. He said "one of you is a devil," referring to the spiritually- blind Judas (John 6:70,71). This was a day or two after Jesus fed the multitude by the miracle of the fishes and the loaves.

In the synagogue at Capernaum Jesus preached His discourse about the "bread from heaven," a message of righteousness by faith. That message caused a terrible shaking among those who followed Him. Those who followed from fear or because of the hope of reward were shaken out, or at least they positioned themselves in such a manner that they could leave at a moment's notice, as Judas did.

Multitudes left Jesus. As He looked around He saw only His twelve bewildered and shaken ministers. He asked them, "Do you also want to go away?" to which Peter replied, "Lord, to whom shall we go? You have the words of eternal life" (John 6:66-68). Eleven of his ministers came through the terrible ordeal. One did not. Judas rejected the spiritual food Christ gave. He refused Christ's gift of righteousness. He spurned and rejected it. Like Esau centuries earlier, he sold his spiritual birthright for a mess of temporal pottage.

From that time until he betrayed Christ, Judas brought confusion into the ranks of Christ's ministers. Jesus never openly rebuked Judas until the night when Judas got angry as Mary washed Christ's feet with precious and very costly ointment. Judas criticized Mary for wasting money (that he coveted). But Jesus told him straight, "Let her alone." Immediately after this, Judas, smarting from Christ's only rebuke to him, went to the priests to negotiate for money in return for his betrayal of Christ (John 12:3-8; Mark 14:6-11).

But later when Jesus was on trial, the conscience smitten Judas confessed his sin and asked for the release of Jesus. But it was too late. The priests who caballed with him in private now spurned him in public (see Matthew 27:3-5). But his friend, Jesus, whom he betrayed, pitied him and did not reproach him.

If Judas had searched the psalms to learn about Jesus and His mission, he would have learned of his own weaknesses, and he could have been strengthened and healed. Instead of centuries of abhorrence that have followed him, he might be remembered along with the other eleven leaders as a teacher of righteousness. Even so, and in spite of what he did to Him, Jesus loved him to the end. Amazing love! Amazing grace!

# Chapter 7

## A Prayer of Faith and Investigation: Psalm 17, and Christ was Raised From the Dead in Fulfillment of Psalm 16

Psalm 17 is a prayer of invitation for investigation. Study it in the light of the innocent Christ, numbered with the transgressors. He was tested by the closest scrutiny of God ("examined," verse 3, margin), God could find nothing in Christ. He was innocent. He knew no sin. Even His enemies could find no sin in Him through which they could convict Him (John 8:46).

Another tested Christ. Lucifer examined Him, to see if he could find a flaw in His character. Since God's searching eye "found nothing" in Christ, the devil's investigation was an exercise in futility. Jesus testified that "he has nothing in Me" (John 14:30). This has to do with sins. The devil could find "not even one" sin in Him. Nothing in Christ responded to the devil's temptations.

The reason for Christ's flawless character is found in the fact that He would do "not even one" thing of Himself (John 5:19,30). Christ's words and works were done by the Father's power (John 14:10). This is living by faith, righteousness by faith.

Christ was a servant of the grace of God, and it was thereby impossible for Him to be forced into sin so long as He remained under God's power. Grace is always greater than sin! The Spirit that dwelt within Christ was stronger than the inherited tendencies of sinful flesh (Romans 5:20, 21; 6:16; Galatians 5:16, 17). Thus it was God, in Christ, who condemned sin in the flesh (Romans 8:3).

This should greatly encourage your heart, especially as you face the judgment. To the condition of Christ when He was on earth, in human flesh, God will bring His people in the faith of Jesus. The devil will find "not even one" sin in them by which he might gain the advantage. The reason he will find nothing in God's people is because first God Himself will examine them. Because of the power of His grace dwelling in them and the righteousness of Christ given to them, He will find nothing in them! Judgment will be pronounced in their favor. The everlasting gospel message will accomplish God's work in the believer (Revelation 14:12; 18:1; Daniel 7:9, 10, 22; 1 Thessalonians 5:8, 9).

After God's examination, then and only then, will Satan have opportunity to investigate God's elect. No doubt the devil will try them to the uttermost. But he will meet with the same result that he did with Christ, for Christ is formed within them as the hope of glory. The same righteousness of God that was in Christ and given to them, Satan will test. He will find "not one thing" that will respond to his sophistry. This is so because God's grace will have such control over God's people that sin in them will be conquered and condemned in their sinful flesh by the power of His word and the indwelling of His Holy Spirit based upon the work of Christ on the cross.

While on the one hand the law of God points out sin in the lives of everyone, it also testifies in behalf of the believer (Romans 3:20, 21). Only Christ's righteousness will be found in God's people (Jeremiah 23:6). God's law of righteousness will testify to the genuineness of that righteousness. God has already investigated that flawless righteousness in Christ. As Christ could do nothing of Himself, so His followers "can do not one thing" of themselves (John 5:19, 30; 15:5). Christ only will be seen in the believer. Christ and His mind, His thoughts, His words, His works, His righteousness.

Christ purposed in His mind not to transgress with His lips (Psalm 17:3; 1 Peter. 2:22). So it is with His people (Revelation 14:5; 1 Peter 3:10; James 2:26; 3:1-12). By God's word, Christ was kept from sin (Psalm 17:4; Matthew 4:4). So it must be with His people (Psalm 119:19).

In Psalm 17:5-15 we read the prayer of faith. Since Christ lived "by every word that proceeded out of the mouth of God" we can be assured that He made this psalm His own. He endured the cross, despising its shame (Hebrews 12:2-4). The psalm ends in faith: "As for me, I will see Your face in righteousness; I shall be satisfied when I awake in Your likeness." From this, let's turn our attention to Psalm 16.

It was written by David. No doubt some of this psalm is about his own experience. But it is another of the psalms *about* Christ. It concludes with the hope of His resurrection. His prayer of faith here is that He would not experience corruption in the grave. This can only apply to Christ and not to David because it is evident from Peter's sermon on the day of Pentecost, and later from Paul's sermon in the synagogue in Pisidia that this refers to Jesus (Acts 2:25-35; 13:33-37).

Psalm 16:8-11 is a recorded prayer of the faith of Jesus concerning His resurrection. Peter in his sermon on the day of Pentecost quoted this passage in reference to the outpouring of the Holy Spirit on that day. He told the "men of Israel" that although they had put Christ to death, God raised Him up in fulfillment of this psalm (Acts 2:24-32). Verse 10 is quoted directly in Acts 2:27 (KJV): "Thou wilt not leave My soul in hell, neither wilt Thou suffer Thine Holy One to see corruption." Peter argued that this referred to Christ, and not to David, because David did see corruption and he was still on earth in his tomb in Jerusalem at the time Peter preached to the people on the day of Pentecost.

Christ went to hell for us (Psalm 16:10). *Sheol* in the Old Testament and *Hades* in the New meant the grave. Christ died. Both soul and body died. Isaiah wrote that His "soul" would be made "an offering for sin," and that "He poured out

His soul unto death, and was numbered with the transgressors" (Isaiah 53:10, 12).

### Christ's death was more than physical.

Had His death been only physical, it would have been no more than a pagan sacrifice. But no! He *really* died. His total mortal person perished. When He died, His thoughts perished, just as they do with all who die (Psalm 146:4). He died the equivalent of what the Bible calls the "second death" (Revelation 20:6). This death is punishment for sin. This is what mankind earns. This death is "good-bye" forever to life. It means eternal separation from God. But our "wages" were paid by Jesus. "The wages of sin is death" even the death of Jesus. Because Jesus lived fully by faith, and in faith of God's promise to bring Him back from the dead, He was resurrected from the grave and now ever lives to make intercession for us. Because He died, you live. Because He died you may live forever, conditioned of course on your non-resistance to His grace.

Christ in his human nature is the only human who was destined to go to hell. No other human being *has* to go there. That fire was prepared for devils, not mankind. Those only who persistently refuse the grace of God that surrounds them just as certainly as the atmosphere encircles the earth, will join the devil and his angels there (Matthew 25:41).

# Chapter 8

## The Conflict Between the Senses and Faith
## Psalm 42

ere we have a mirror into the psyche of mankind in the battle with depression that comes upon all from time to time. In this psalm we witness the deep depression that came to David as it comes to many sons and daughters of Adam.

Later in the chapter we observe the triumph of faith. It ends as it begins. This song begins with faith and its holy desires toward God and communion with Him (verses 1, 2). But between the beginning and the ending there is despair and sorrow of heart. This is a window into the kind of sorrow through which Jesus, the Man of Sorrows, passed.

In verse 3 we observe the depression affecting David's appestat, the area of the brain that regulates appetite and food intake. Verses 3 through 6 reveal the fierce struggle between depression and faith.

"My tears have been my food day and night, while they continually say to me, 'Where is your God?' When I remember these things, I pour out my soul within me. For I used to go with the multitude; I went with them to the house of God, with the voice of joy and praise, with a multitude that kept a pilgrim feast. Why are you cast down,

O my soul? And why are you disquieted within in? Hope in God, for I shall yet praise Him for the help of his countenance. O my God, my soul is cast down within me."

A true psychological statement is declared in verse 3. Loss of appetite is often brought on by depression. Because his emotions became depressed, food became repulsive to David. He wrote that he lived on his tears—they were his food 24 hours a day. David the king tended to swing to extremes emotionally. He experienced great highs from time to time, but when he was down, he was really down. Those tendencies were passed on to his offspring.

A deep state of depression is again depicted in verses 10 and 11:

"I will say to my Rock, 'Why have You forgotten me?' As with a breaking of my bones, my enemies reproach me, while they say to me all day long, 'Where is your God?' Why are you cast down, O my soul? And why are you disquieted within me?"

From the inspired record we learn that depression overtook several of God's chosen leaders. Three examples will be given here: Jonah, Elijah, and Moses.

Jonah's depression came upon him because of his resistance to the Holy Spirit. In his anger and despondency he asked God to end his life: "Therefore now, O Lord, please take my life from me, for it is better for me to die than to live!" (Jonah 4:3; see also verses 8 and 9).

Jonah, the reluctant prophet, got himself into this state of mind because he did not want to go to Nineveh to warn the inhabitants of their evil ways and to call them to repentance and faith. He was angry with God because He was so merciful to the Ninevite "heathens." Jonah wanted God to belie His character and destroy the Ninevites from sheer vindictiveness. He did not care for those people. He found no comfort in their salvation. But in Nineveh there were 60,000 persons more in tune with God than His sulking prophet!

Elijah on the other hand had just completed a great work for God on Mount Carmel. There he overthrew the worship of Baal and deposed the false prophets. God's people, including the king, were deeply impressed with the preaching of Elijah that day. Elijah, although exhausted from the activity of the day, was jubilant. He was sure that the people had turned back to God. Perhaps he hoped that even Jezebel would be convinced. But alas, she became furious and threatened to execute him within 24 hours. Seized with terror that led to deep depression, Elijah lost his bearings, bolted and fled for his life.

**After traveling a day's journey he sat down utterly depressed and prayed to die.**

"It is enough!" he said. "Now, Lord, take my life, for I am no better than my fathers!" (1 Kings 19:4). Self-worth at an all-time low, he longed for the grave.

**But notice how God cared for him when he could not think rationally.**

He let Elijah rest while an angel prepared food for him, awakened him, then told him to eat and drink, which he did. Then again he lay down, and slept some more. Again later, the angel came to him, touched him, told him a second time to eat, and to be on his way.

Elijah traveled for forty more days, arriving at Mount Sinai. There he hid himself in the dark recesses of a cave. God then came to Elijah, asking questions of him. He reminded God of his zeal and good works for Him. He felt he was all alone. Everyone was against him (verses 10, 13). He thought all of Israel was against him. But in reality only one was—the apostate queen. In this condition of despondency Elijah pled "with God *against* Israel" (Romans 11:2, 3), the very people God sent him to save!

In love and tenderness God dealt with His despondent prophet. He spoke to him in "a still small voice" (verse 12). The literal meaning of that phrase is, "a delicate whispering voice." This is what Elijah needed. Today persons in despondency and depression need to hear that "delicate whispering voice."

Moses also suffered from severe depression that led to despair. This came upon him because of the pressure of administrative duties. This pressure came from the people because of several events. In Numbers 11 the problem was murmuring over food. The people grew tired of the diet God gave them. They "lusted for the flesh pots of Egypt." They murmured and complained to Moses. In desperation he also complained to God, not about the food, but because he felt that God had laid burdens of government upon him too heavy to be carried: "Why have You afflicted Your servant? And why have I not found favor in Your sight, that You have laid the burden of all these people on me?" (Numbers 11:11).

In his despondency and depression, Moses continued, "I am not able to bear all these people alone, because the burden is too heavy for me. If You treat me like this, please kill me here and now! ..." God then instructed Moses to delegate his responsibilities. God assured him that He would be with the seventy officers chosen to take over some of his administrative duties.

**Some people feel that depression is a sin. It can be, but in and of itself it is not.**

Sinning can lead to depression, but all depression does not come from sinning. Depression may be related to several factors such as one's physical makeup and body chemistry, or glandular functions. Emotional patterns and personality structure may enter into the problem. Or learned-feeling concepts can produce depression. Circumstances that bring on anxiety and stress can produce depression. The guilt of sin from known disobedience definitely drags one down into this mental state. I am not talking about a general sense of guilt. Usually a general sense of guilt is a pseudo-guilt, a false guilt.

When God deals with sin in the life of an individual, He is very specific. He points out the sin that needs to be confessed that the guilt may be removed so the person may be comforted (see John 16:7-9). A general sense of guilt without known sin comes from another source—either from the enemy or from a falsely educated conscience.

There are things that can be done by an individual in meeting depression. Avoid being alone. Seek help from others (who are helpful and joyful). Sing. Singing lifts the spirits. So does praising God and giving thanks. Read the psalms out loud. Learn to lean on God's promises. Rest confidently in the presence of God's comforting Spirit (Psalm 42:5).

**Problems need to be faced squarely.**

Accept whatever responsibility you have in the matter. By Christ's grace, forgive everyone involved in your problem, including yourself. As Christ asked for forgiveness for those who crucified Him (Luke 23:24), He gives grace and faith to us today to enable us to pray that prayer. His prayer of forgiveness included you also.

A question you need to ask yourself is this: Do you really want to be healed? Some persons do not want to be. They like to feel depressed and low. They want to depend on the chemical reactions and stimuli in their nervous system caused by anger and/or depression. Those feelings are familiar to them through habitual indulgence in self-pity. Others like to feel angry. And yet others like to feel sorry for themselves. So ask yourself the question, "Do I really want to be healed?" Then ask the Holy Spirit to show you what the real problem is, and how you need to pray about it. He will help. He will direct. He will comfort (Romans 8:26; John 16:7).

**We want to return to Elijah's and Moses' experiences of depression.**

Elijah had been so mentally low that he prayed to die. From that deep depression he recovered. God's goodness led him to exercise faith, and he came out of his mental state of despondency and despair. Not only did God bring him out of his depression, *He translated him*. Elijah did not die. He was taken to heaven.

It is of special interest to note that Elijah along with Moses (the first one to be raised from the grave) were sent from heaven to give encouragement to Jesus shortly before He went through His mental agony in Gethsemane and on Calvary. They "spoke of His death which He was about to accomplish at Jerusalem " (Luke 9:30, 31).

Moses was the first to be resurrected from the dead. "Death reigned from Adam to Moses." Satan, the self-appointed warden over the grave, claimed it as his prison house. His claim had the appearance of truth. For millennia no one was set free. He fought fiercely to keep Moses incarcerated in the tomb. But Michael the Archangel simply rebuked Satan and called Moses back to life (Romans 5:14; Jude 9).

Moses encouraged Jesus by his testimony and his presence. To see and hear the resurrected Moses must have given Jesus reassurance, hope, and confidence. Jesus knew He must "taste death for everyone." He must die the death of the damned, "the wages" of our sin. He must die the equivalent of the "second death" (Hebrews 2:9; Romans 6:23; Revelation 20:6).

Before and during the dying process, Christ was to experience to the fullest degree the depths of the feelings of depression, despondency, and despair as the full weight of sin rested upon His nervous system. His heart ruptured from the experience. His mind nearly shattered as sin rent and tore it with a force greater than the earthquake that ripped rocks from their foundations as He died.

So Elijah and Moses were sent to bring reassurance, to let Jesus know that by God's grace and by faith in God He would come through the most excruciating experience just ahead. Elijah, formerly troubled mentally and later translated, encouraged Jesus in the closing hours of His life on earth.

**As Jesus entered the garden of Gethsemane, the weight of sin began to crush Him.**

In Mark 14:33 we have recorded for us the state of mind experienced by Christ. "He began to be troubled and deeply distressed." He was in terrible turbulence. The word "troubled" is not found in Matthew's account of Gethsemane, but is very significant. It indicates something of the horror of the great darkness that fell upon Abraham (Genesis 15:12), but worse and much more frightful.

Never had man experienced such terrifying sorrow as that which came upon Christ. Never before had Christ experienced anything like this. Depression and despair coming suddenly upon Him at this time terrified Him. He trembled. The terror was grounded internally as He was "made to be sin" for you and me. He was made to serve with our sins, and was thus wearied with our iniquities. He was made "a curse" for us (Galatians 3:13). The curse of mankind was transferred to Him as our Bondsman, our Surety, our Representative.

Writing of Christ's distress, Mark chose a word meaning *deep* depression. Jesus felt the heaviness that comes in depression. As Christ gave Himself in exchange for our sins, those sins became His. Never did He commit sin. Never! But He felt as though He had.

David captured the depression of Christ brought on by sin in these words: "For innumerable evils have surrounded Me; My iniquities have overtaken Me, so that I am not able to look up; they are more than the hairs of My head; therefore My heart fails Me" (Psalm 40:12). Full of anxiety, anguish and sorrow, Christ was depressed and dejected.

Staggering like a drunken man and nearly falling, Jesus exclaimed, "My soul is exceedingly sorrowful, even to death" (Mark 14:34). That sorrow of mind nigh unto death forced Him into a fetal position as He lay trembling on the ground (verse 45). Tormented with our sin and guilt, He tasted death for all mankind and abolished the curse. The tasting of the death is not to be construed to mean that He merely put it to His lips and sampled it. He *drank* the cup of death to its last dregs in Gethsemane and on Calvary.

Christ was in perilous mental agony as our sins rested so heavy upon His soul. In this state of mind, bloody sweat was forced from the pores of His body and moistened the ground where He lay in tormenting agony. Christ is the Alpha and Omega of depression and sorrow. Because Christ went through this excruciating experience, you can know that He understands you when you go through unexplainable mental pain. You may draw comfort from this.

During those times you can simply rest in His care and keeping. You may not be able to pray because of despair. Your mind may be clouded because of depression. Then don't try to think. Jesus loves you. Your infirmities are understood by Him. Simply rest in His care and keeping. He will bring you through your terrible ordeal. He has never lost a battle, and He never will.

Our Savior's invitation, "Come unto Me, ... and I will give you rest" (Matthew 11:29) is a prescription for the healing of depression, despondency and despair. In Him you may find help because He is the Wonderful Counselor. He has been touched with the "feelings of your infirmities." He knows what kind of and how much help you need. He has been there. He is with you (Isaiah 9:6; Hebrews 4:15; 2:18).

# Chapter 9

# In Confession and Repentance for Sin

# Psalms 31, 38, 40

"Into Thine hand I commit My spirit" (Psalm 31:5, KJV). In this Golgotha psalm is found the last words of Jesus. These are the words of faith, Jesus' prayer of faith. Christ gave Himself up in a special manner to God, the Father. Christ resigned Himself entirely to His keeping. Rather than come down from the cross to save Himself, as He was tempted to do, He was obedient unto death (Matthew 27:39-43; Philippians 2:8). In total submission to and through faith in the Father, Christ died. He voluntarily made Himself an offering for our sins. He died that we might live. He was "made to be sin for us" so "that we might be made the righteousness of God in Him" (2 Corinthians 5:21).

Not only do we have Christ's dying words, we also hear His words in confession in the process of dying:

"Have mercy on Me, O Lord, for I am in trouble; My eye wastes away with grief, Yes, My soul and My body! For My life is spent with grief, and My years with sighing; My strength fails because of My iniquity, and My bones waste away. I am a reproach among all My enemies, but especially among My neighbors, and am repulsive to My acquaintances; those who see outside flee from Me" (verses 9-11).

In previous verses Christ appealed to God's righteousness, and pleaded His relation to Him along with dependence upon Him. Here He appeals to God's mercy. The remembrance Christ makes of His condition is like that of every human being. His troubles were deeply embedded in His mind and nervous system, and made Him a Man of sorrows (Isaiah 53:3-6). So great was Christ's grief, that His very soul was consumed in it, His life was spent by it, and He continually sighed because of it. Christ was intimately acquainted with grief. He was often in tears.

His body was affected with the sorrows of His mind (Psalm 31:10). He confesses sin as though it was His own. This was your sin and my sin in which He had no share, but which He *took* upon Himself as His own. He confesses this sin as though He deserved the affliction that came upon Him. He freely confesses this iniquity as having been the cause of all His trouble. The sense of sin touched Him to the very core of His being, and wasted Him more than all His calamities. Christ's appearance became repulsive to those who looked at Him.

Psalm 38, the third of seven penitential prayers, is typical of the deep sorrow one experiences in heart-felt repentance for sin. Here is witnessed the pouring forth of depressed feelings. Here is seen and felt the distress of mind and body because of sin. Both mental and physical disorientation are described. David, author of this psalm, wrote of his agony because of personal sin. His experience is representative of mankind when convicted of sin.

But more than this, David's experience of repentance foreshadowed Christ's experience when He would be *"made to be sin for us."* David not only was the father of Christ's humanity, he was also a figure or a type of Christ. Jesus experienced soul anguish to a degree that none other can experience, for He took upon Himself all the sins of mankind. This psalm must be studied in the light of Christ's repentance.

In the psalms the Holy Spirit speaks in the person of Christ. In several He testifies in clear words that Christ "has" sin, but it's not His own. These are the words of a suffering Christ as He was *made* guilty for the sins of the world. These are not the words of an innocent person. To study Christ in the psalms is to study Christ the Public Man, the Representative Man, the Corporate Man. He is the second Adam. He became the Head of a race that willed to sin. Christ was "made to be sin for us."

In the first two verses of Psalm 38, arrows as instruments of death symbolize judgment and condemnation. Beginning with verse 3 we read of the condition of human nature: "There is no soundness in my flesh." There is a weakness or a tendency to sin in human nature that comes to everyone through the law of heredity.

**The reality of the awfulness of sin is also described.**

There is "no health in my bones because of my sin" (no *shalom*, no "peace" or cessation from suffering). "Christ suffered for us in the flesh." "He learned obedience from the things which He suffered" (1 Peter 4:1; Hebrews 5:8). Depression affects the bone marrow where most of the white and all the red blood cells are produced. Thus depression affects the body's disease fighting mechanism. "A broken spirit, "writes the wise man, "dries the bones" (Proverbs 17:22).

From where did Christ get sin? The Father "made Him who knew no sin to be sin for us." "All we like sheep have gone astray; we have turned, every one, to his own way; and the Lord has laid on Him the iniquity of us all" (2 Corinthians 5:21; Isaiah 53:6). Christ took our sins as His own. Psalm 38: 4, "My iniquities have gone over My head; like a heavy burden they are too heavy for Me." This verse emphasizes the meaning of verse 3. In Psalm 40:12 we read the prophetic utterance, "They are more than the hairs of My head."

Sin is compared to waters that threaten to drown a person. The unbearable burden of sin is like the pounding waves of the sea. The sin of the world overwhelmed Christ and flooded over His head. This may suggest confusion of thought and dullness of mind from the pain and weight of the guilt of sin. His heart gave out because of this enormous weight of guilt and condemnation caused by sin.

Not all the psalms about Jesus are pleasant pictures concerning Him. Many present Him "touched with the feelings of our infirmities." Our sins became His. They were considered as festering, foul smelling wounds. A more literal reading of Psalm 38:5 is: "My sores have come to stink or smell badly and have decomposed." They are likened to wounds or bruises or as marks from a blow that send forth an offensive putrid odor (compare Isaiah 1:6; 53:5). To "stink" means to give off a strong unpleasant odor. Sin is abhorrent and offensive to Christ who must bear it.

The cross stank. It was a scandal. It represented sin so offensive that it offended or shocked the moral feelings of a community. Christ, made to be sin itself, was an offensive odor to those around Him and loathsome to God. But out of that foul odor comes to us sweet smelling incense, even the righteousness of God.

Christ recognized He was in trouble. Entering into Gethsemane, He staggered like a drunken man. His countenance changed. His thoughts troubled Him. His knees knocked against each other more than did Belshazzar's when he saw the handwriting on the wall. "I am troubled [literally 'bent down'], I am bowed down greatly" (verse 6). He was bent down from depression and heart sickness. There was a convulsive drawing together of His body. He was bent down and sank with sorrow. Especially was this so in His Gethsemane experience. Bent in a fetal position Christ shook with a nameless terror as waves of nausea and panic swept over Him. In that position His internal muscles and organs seemed on fire. An intense burning, like a fever, spread throughout the body (verse 7).

There came over Him an almost total lifelessness, like the rigidity of a corpse. See Him being brought into the condition of a crushing violent dissolution. His groans were more like the roaring of a wild beast than of a man, expressing the raging pain in His mind and soul (verses 8 and 9; compare Psalm 22:1, 2).

Forsaken by family and friend, not one wanted to be associated with Him, while His enemies desired His death (verses 11 and 12; compare Luke 23:21; Deuteronomy 21:23; John 19:7).

In verses 13-16 we read of His response to the charges against Him. He pays no attention to the plots of His enemies. The consciousness of guilt and resignation closes His lips, so that He is not able nor does He wish to refute the false charges of His enemies. He has no counter-evidence by which to vindicate Himself. In the consciousness of imputed sin He is obliged to be silent, and renouncing all self-help, He abandons His cause to God. Here we observe "the faith *of* Jesus."

**Next we read of His repentance.**

Mental pain and alarm, anxiety, fear and terror, all are depicted in the following passage: "I am ready to fall, and my sorrow is continually before me" (Psalm 38:17). "Surely He has borne our iniquities and carried our sorrows. ... He was wounded for our transgressions, He was bruised for our iniquities; the chastisement for our peace was upon Him, and by His stripes we are healed" (Isaiah 53:4, 5).

In the six months preceding the baptism of Jesus, the preaching of John the Baptizer stirred Judah. Many came to be baptized by him. They came in repentance, "confessing their sins" (Matthew 3:6). Others went through the motions of repentance and confession in order to become part of that growing movement of believers who anticipated the soon coming of the expected Messiah. With keen spiritual eyesight, John called on those so-called professors to bring forth fruits of repentance.

Jesus also at the call of God made His way to where John was baptizing. As Jesus took the steps in conversion preceding baptism—repentance and faith, John held back from baptizing Him. John sensed the purity of this Man. He felt he should be baptized by Jesus. Christ then spoke to John of the importance of doing this. "Permit it to be so now, for thus it is fitting for us to fulfill all righteousness" (Matthew 3:15).

True repentance has faith within itself. While the convicted but believing mind despairs of itself, it does not do so of God. So it was with Christ.

Psalm 38:18 records, "I confess my iniquity; I am sorry for my sin" (NRSV). Christ was fully conscious of the guilt and punishment of sin unto death. He reaped man's sowing. Strength of life, prosperity, good health comes to the wicked, but weakness and death to Christ. This is what Christ chose when He decided to become a human being.

## But was not Christ innocent?

Personally, yes. But when He became flesh, He became guilty, condemned, and subject to the curse *as He took the place of mankind.* "And the Lord hath laid on Him the iniquity of us all" (Isaiah 53:6). All the committed sins of the world were placed upon Him. And through the law of heredity, sin in its tendency was also laid upon Him.

Because He took upon Himself our fallen nature, His righteous character had to be by faith. The righteousness of Jesus was not by human nature, but by faith alone. Christ always followed that which is good (Psalm 38:20). This was the reason for the intense hatred against Him. Man could only stand three and a half years of His faith-righteousness. They rendered evil for His sinless life.

Christ's life of righteousness by faith was a stumbling block during and after His personal mission on earth. It was a stumbling block for His family and for His people. Family members attempted to break His faith in God. But Christ refused to follow them in evil.

In Psalm 38:21,22 we read His last appeal. He closed His petitions with sighs of agony for help. But none came. Christ died as He lived—with faith. Christ's life was one of faith. He was born by faith. He was sanctified by faith. In short, He lived by faith. And Christ writhing in the agonies of death, died in faith.

Psalm 40 predicts the coming of Christ into the world to do God's will: "Burnt offerings and sin offering You did not require. Then I said, 'Behold, I come; in the scroll of the Book it is written of Me. I delight to do Your will, O My God'" (Psalm 40:6-8). Hebrews 10:5-9 verifies Christ in this psalm:

> "Sacrifice and offering You did not desire, but a body You have prepared for Me. In burnt offerings and sacrifices for sin You had no pleasure. Then I said 'Behold, I have come—in the volume of the book it is written of Me—to do Your will, O God.' Previously saying, 'Sacrifice and offering, burnt offerings, and offerings for sin You did not desire, nor had pleasure in them' (which are offered according to the law), then He said, 'Behold, I have come to do Your will, O God.' He takes away the first that He may establish the second."

Psalm 40 predicted Christ's voluntary submission to the Father's will in the words: "Sacrifice and offering You did not desire; My ears You have opened" (verse 6). Exodus 21:1-6 records the relationship between a voluntary slave and his master. After serving a certain number of years, the slave was to go free during the year of release. But if he chose to stay, the master bore a hole through his ear. This signified that the servant's ears would always remain open to the command of the master. The servant would always obey. In coming to this earth Christ took the form of a servant. In our human nature His ears were always open to obey the word of God. And through His obedience we are made righteous (Romans 5:19).

**Christ delighted to do the Father's will because His law was written on His heart.**

And when we are born from above we are brought into harmony with God's law. Never are we justified by obedience to the law; neither are we justified from keeping it; but we are justified in order to obey it. Justification by faith carries the law of God on the face of it. This justification is the law incarnate in Christ and then placed in us by grace when we accept Christ. To be made righteous means to be brought into harmony with God's law of righteousness.

We see clearly that the Holy Spirit applied Psalm 40 to Christ. Christ is pictured as taking our sins as His own. This is what broke His heart.

> "I delight to do Your will, O My God, and Your law is within My heart. I have proclaimed the good news of righteousness in the great congregation; indeed, I do not restrain my lips, O Lord, You Yourself know. I have not hidden Your righteousness within My heart; I have declared Your faithfulness and Your salvation; I have not concealed Your lovingkindness and Your truth from the great congregation. Do not withhold Your tender mercies from Me, O Lord; let Your lovingkindness and Your truth continually preserve Me. For innumerable evils have surrounded me; My iniquities have overtaken Me, so that I am not able to look up; they are more than the hairs of My head; therefore My heart fails Me" (verses 8-12).

Christ did not sin, but He *took* ours as His own. Christ gave Himself for our sins (Galatians 1:4). "The Lord hath laid upon Him the iniquity of us all" (Isaiah 53:6). Because of the pressure and stress of the burden of the guilt and condemnation from our sins that were laid upon Him, His heart gave out. Our iniquities, which He took as His own, were more than the number of the hairs on His sacred head. And although He could not look up because of the weight of those sins, yet the faith of Jesus was triumphant. In the verses that follow we read the praises that poured forth from the mouth of Jesus:

"Be pleased, O Lord, to deliver Me; O Lord, make haste to help Me! Let them be ashamed and brought to mutual confusion who seek to destroy My life; let them be driven backward and brought to dishonor who wish Me evil. Let them be appalled because of their shame, who say to Me, 'Aha, aha!' Let all who seek You rejoice and be glad in You; let such as love Your salvation say continually, 'The Lord be magnified!' but I am poor and needy; yet the Lord thinks upon Me. You are My help and My deliverer; do not delay, O My God" (Psalm 40:13-17).

From this we may learn that because Christ was made to be sin for us, God will not turn from any person whose iniquities are more than the hairs of his head! To the one who is burdened down with guilt and condemnation from personal sin, Christ offers to take the weary load. He understands from experience what it means to feel guilty and condemned.

# Chapter 10

## Another Psalm of Repentance

## Psalm 69

After Psalm 22, Psalm 69 is referred to in the New Testament more times than any of the others. John 15:25 quotes Psalm 69:4 as the fulfillment of Christ's experience of being hated "without cause." The disciples remembered verse seven of this passage as being fulfilled when Jesus cleansed the temple: "Because zeal for Your house has eaten me up" (see John 2:17). The reproach and shame of Christ were predicted in Psalm 69:7 and 9 (compare Romans 15:3).

Christ as Surety for the human race is presented in Psalm 69:4: "Though I have stolen nothing, I still must restore it." A surety is a bondsman, one who places money or possessions in behalf of another who has been legally charged with a crime, but awaits his trial. The bondsman in placing his money or possessions, makes himself responsible for the failure of the person charged with a crime to show up for trial. Christ as our Surety pledged His life for the failure of mankind. He became responsible for Adam's failure. He pledged Himself to restore that which He had not done.

Christ took the place of Adam as the Federal Head of the human race. He took Adam's sin in which He had no share that Adam and we might partake of His righteousness. Christ ran the fearful risk of losing everything in undertaking the work of redeeming man. He became us in all things that we might be saved. Our sins became His because He became our Surety.

Christ experienced what the sinner experiences to the fullest extent, when weighted down with sin and guilt. As He "was made to be sin" He felt what we feel when we give in to sin. He knows true sorrow for sin.

When Adam sinned against known light, the entire race that was to come from him was doomed to condemnation and everlasting destruction. Had Adam died then as he should have, you and I would never have seen the light of day. But God had a plan for us. He made Himself responsible for man's failure. He became Surety for the whole race. This is the reason why "we see Jesus, who was made a little lower than the angels, for the suffering of death ..." He became "the Lamb slain from he foundation of the world" (Revelation 13:8). The altar of sacrifice and the promise of redemption were placed side by side in the beginning (Genesis 3:15; 4:4). Each sheds light on the other concerning Christ and Him crucified.

In the psalms the Holy Spirit speaks in the person of Christ. In several He testifies in clear words that Christ *has* sin—our sin. These are the words of a suffering Christ as He was "made" to be guilty for the sins of the world; as He was "made to be sin" itself for us! He is the second and last Adam. He became the Head of a race that willed to sin.

## Psalm 69 begins with a figure of calamity:

"Save Me, O God! for the waters have come up to My neck. I sink in deep mire, where there is no standing; I have come into deep waters, where the floods overflow Me. I am weary with My crying; My throat is dry; My eyes fail while I wait for My God" (verses 1-3).

Then verse 5: "O God, You know My foolishness; and My sins are not hidden from You." What a picture of Christ here, repenting and confessing sin! In this is our assurance. In Christ's repentance, in Christ's confession our repentance, our confession is complete. After confessing your sins as thoroughly as you know how, have you wondered if your confession was good enough?

After asking an audience that question I observed the tear streaked faces of a man and his wife and heard their answer: "Yes, every day!" I pointed out that our confession of sin falls short in and of itself. But thank God there is One that did not. Your sincere heartfelt repentance and confessions are made complete in Christ's perfect repentance and confession. He took our sins and repented of them and confessed them as if He had committed them. Never in any way did Christ sin. If He would have sinned, there would be no hope for us or for Himself. But our sins were laid upon Him. He was numbered with the transgressors (Isaiah 53:4-6, 12). Christ and Him crucified means Christ crucified for us.

**Another practical aspect is found in this psalm.**

Were you ever rejected by close friends or relatives? In verse 8 we read the prophetic word concerning Christ's non-acceptance by immediate family members. "I have become a stranger to My brothers, and an alien to My mother's children." Family members became enemies of the cross of Christ! These did not know what Christ was doing. At one time they thought He had lost His mind. As they learned of some of Christ's activities  of ordaining His twelve disciples and of healing the sick, Mark recorded their reaction: "But when His own people heard about this, they went out to lay hold on Him: for they said, He is out of His mind" (Mark 3:2).

About one year before Christ was crucified, His brothers mocked him with unbelief. A "shaking" occurred within the followers of Christ. Many left Him. In Judea Jews sought to kill Him and He departed from there and returned to Galilee. At the time of the Feast of Tabernacles Christ's brothers in unbelief said "Depart from here and go into Judea, that Your disciples also may see the work that You are doing. For no one does anything in secret while he himself seeks to be known openly. If You do these things, show Yourself to the world" (John 7:3, 4). John added, "For even His brothers did not believe on Him" (verse 5). Christ's enemies included members of His own household. But there is some good news.

*Calvary made peace within that family.* It created friends out of enemies. As far as a person in his carnal state is concerned, the cross is totally foreign to him. The natural man hates the cross. There are no friends of the cross. But the cross *creates* faith. It makes friends out of enemies. Jesus' own brothers who hated Him became His friends through the cross. We find them listed among the disciples who gathered together in the upper room in Jerusalem after Jesus ascended to heaven (Acts 1:14). One of His brothers, James, became the presiding leader of the early church (Acts 15:13; Galatians 1:18, 19).

If there are problems of alienation and animosity in your family, consider studying the closing scenes of Christ's life together and see if the cross will unite the family again. The cross is the great center of attraction for the world. It makes friends out of enemies. It creates hope. The cross is a revelation of God's goodness and grace to us while at the same time it caused infinite grief to Him and to His Son Jesus Christ.

Because Christ was made to be sin, the mental anguish from sin broke His heart. Psalm 69:20, 21 reveals to us that experience: "Reproach has broken My heart, and I am full of heaviness; I looked for someone to take pity, and there was none; and for comforters, but I found none." Christ longed for comfort, but no one—no disciple, no friend, no relative would or could comfort Him. A pagan soldier in mercy offered Jesus a pain killer.

"They also gave Me gall for My food, and for My thirst they gave Me vinegar to drink" (Matthew 27:33-46). Christ was tempted to use a drug. This was a fearful temptation. He needed something to drink from the loss of body fluids that occurred because of the activities of the previous grueling hours of interrogation and physical abuse. He had not slept for approximately thirty hours.

Without a doubt, Christ was fearfully tempted to bite down on that sponge filled with vinegar to ease the pain and to relieve a bit of His physical need for liquid. But as soon as that sponge  touched His lips, He turned from it, refusing any temporary "fix." He could not afford to allow any possibility of having His mind clouded in those crucial hours of agony.

## Satan's dreaded hour arrived.

The battle raged between these two princes. The stakes were enormous. All the pent-up fires of hell burst upon Christ on the cross. But the enemy could not induce Christ to sin, neither could he force Him. Christ's faith and mind held fast to God during that fearful struggle. After describing the judgments to come upon those who betrayed and crucified Christ, this psalm then ends in the triumph of faith and praise (verses 30-36).

# Chapter 11

# And Yet Another Penitential Psalm

# Psalm 51

This psalm is David's recorded confession and prayer for forgiveness of his personal sin. This experience came after Nathan the prophet went to him because of David's grievous sin of adultery with Bathsheba and the murder of her husband, Uriah the Hittite, the faithful military officer.

Verse 5 is a clear statement of the kind of human nature inherited by David at conception. He inherited tendencies through the ancestral line of Judah and beyond, reaching back to Jacob and to Abraham. Jacob was a deceiver. Judah was deceitful, and a man of licentious conduct whose children were born of a woman who had been his daughter-in-law and who played the part of a harlot to get him to fulfill a former promise to her after her first husband died. From the beginning of David's ancestral line, the tendency to immorality was cultivated and strengthened in succeeding generations.

For several years, while under grace, David was kept from giving in to ancestral hereditary weaknesses. However, successes both politically and militarily contributed to elevating himself in his thinking. No worldly empire could stand before him. His armies were always victorious in war. A few battles were lost, but never a war. As he departed from total dependence on God's grace, he felt he was strong enough to resist temptations that came both from without and from within his fallen human nature. This was the fatal flaw in his thinking. His hereditary nature, like quicksand, sucked him into the quagmire of sin.

## David was no match for the infirmities of his fallen flesh.

With greater force than the suction of a modern jet engine, which is able to pull a person into its chamber of death, David was pulled into sin by the power of inherited tendencies to sin because he turned from God's grace.

Then, under the conviction of his sin and consequently in the depths of despair and despondency, David prayed for forgiveness, for restoration and peace with God (Psalm 51:1-9). His prayer for renewal is recorded in verses 10-13. Here is David's struggle to gain inward assurance that his sin was forgiven as announced to him by Nathan the prophet, and after repenting of his sin of adultery with Bathsheba. His vow of spiritual sacrifice is given in verses 14-17. He ends with intercessory prayer for Jerusalem, verses 18, 19.

Although David wrote this psalm because of his personal sin with Bathsheba against Uriah and God, yet it is of general use for all repentant persons as is the case with most all other psalms. It is penitential in context, expressing the deep desires of all repentant hearts. Nevertheless, this is a record of David's repentance for his personal sin. And it was to be sung in the public service of the congregation.

David sinned against several people, including his family, and against the people of God, as well as against Uriah and Bathsheba. But none of these were sinned against as much as was God. David realized the gravity of the situation, and so his repentance was deep and heart-felt.

## Repentance and confession give honor to God.

God is justified in His threats against sin. Heartfelt repentance and confession clear God when He is judged and when He executes His judgments. David recorded this confession that when he should come into trouble, none could blame

God, or that He had done David any wrong. All who are truly repentant justify God by condemning themselves and asking for God's forgiveness (Psalm 51:1-4).

In verse 5 David writes about his origin. He confesses the undoneness of his fallen human nature. Had David considered this before, he would not have given in to the temptation, nor have ventured upon enchanted ground. His sin might have been prevented had he seriously considered his inherited weaknesses.

His tendencies led him into sin against Bathsheba, Uriah, his family, and God. Once he allowed the desires of the flesh to control him, thus separating from grace, he could not help himself. Not only was David guilty of adultery and murder, he had an adulterous and murderous nature which he inherited from his ancestors.

Tendencies to sin are twisted in with human nature as it passes from one generation to the next through the genes, by the law of heredity. David's mother and father came into the world with sinful fallen human nature. From conception David had the snares of sin within the flesh. Inherited fallen nature is a burden to all believers and the ruin of all unbelievers.

**The call of God to the fallen race is a call to repentance and to faith.**

God desires to remove from us the offenses we have committed and to give us new hearts. Not only does He command and invite us to repent, He gives us the very words by which we may return to Him: "Take words with you, and return to the Lord. Say to Him, 'Take away all iniquity; receive us graciously, for we will offer the sacrifices of our lips'" (Hosea 14:2).

David's sin is not an exception to the human family. His sin is rampant in the world today. If ever he needed saving from sin, we today need it in a hundred-fold degree more. Both young and old need the help of an outside power. We desperately need a Savior who understands our weaknesses and who will come nigh to us. Is there such a One? Yes. He is the "Seed of David." It is to Him we now turn.

An echo of Psalm 40:6 is found in Psalm 51:16: "You do not desire sacrifice, or else I would give it; you do not delight in burnt offering." This thought is repeated in Hebrews 10:5, 6 in reference to Christ: "Sacrifice and offering You did not desire, but a body You have prepared for Me. In burnt offerings and sacrifices for sin You had no pleasure." In Psalm 51:17 we find the acceptable offering: "The sacrifices of God are a broken spirit, a broken and a contrite heart—these, O God, You will not despise." This was the sacrifice Christ offered.

Christ, the second Adam, the "Man of Sorrows," became "acquainted with grief" in order to represent us. Christ *for us* was Christ *as us* and *with us*. "Numbered with the transgressors," "He poured out his soul" in repentance "unto death" (Isaiah 53:3,12).

The Book of Psalms takes in the whole of Christ's life as our Representative, the Son of Man on earth. The ending of His life by way of the cross is found in Psalm 51:17, "The sacrifices of God are a broken spirit, a broken heart—these, O God, You will not despise." The marginal reading of the NIV gives it in the first person: "My sacrifice, O God, is" a broken spirit. Christ's contrite and broken heart God did not despise. The bruising of the heel of the promised Seed of Genesis 3:15 involved the breaking of Christ's heart in unspeakable anguish. Hodgkin wrote that Christ is the prophetic subject in Psalm 51:17:

> "By wicked hands He was crucified and slain. By the determinate counsel and foreknowledge of God He was delivered to death. By His own will He laid down His life. These three statements are all true in the mystery of that great sacrifice for sin.
>
> "Surely we have in Psalm li. not merely the cry of the sinner, but a prophecy of this great sacrifice in the words: 'The sacrifices of God are

a broken spirit: a broken and a contrite heart, O God, Thou wilt not despise' (li. 17). This is 'the plural of majesty.' In Hebrew the plural is often put where the word great is to be understood.

"'The great sacrifice of God is a broken heart.' This was the sacrifice that our Saviour offered for us. He clothed Himself in a human body that He might have it to offer (Heb. x. 5, 9, 10). He became possessed of a human heart that it might be broken. The way into the holiest is opened up for us through the broken heart of our Saviour.

"This is the gospel for us sinners. It is this that humbles us and brings us to know the power of the cross of Christ to break the power of sin and set us free to serve Him" (A.M. Hodgkin, *Christ in All the Scriptures,* Pickering & Inglis, London, Eighth Edition, 1936, p. 119).

Psalm 51:5: "Behold, I was brought forth in iniquity, and in sin did my mother conceive me" reveals the fallenness of human nature into which David was born. This Scripture, by extension is testifying beforehand of the sufferings of Christ. Throughout the psalms there is plainly stated for us the kind of human nature Christ *took* when He was conceived in the womb of His mother Mary.

## This penitential psalm was indited by the Spirit of God.

Every repentant human being has uttered the sentiments, if not the words, of this inspired prayer, including Jesus. Christ was the Son of David. He was the "Seed of David." He was the promised "fruit" of David. This truth is the gospel of God. ... "[T]he gospel of God ... [is] concerning His Son Jesus Christ our Lord, who was born of the seed of David according to the flesh" (Romans 1:1-3). "From this man's [David's] seed, according to the promise, God raised up for Israel a Savior—Jesus" (Acts 13:23; see also Acts 2:30). This was in fulfillment of God's promise to David that the Messiah would be the fruit of his body (see Psalm 132:11).

Modern science has discovered that along with physical attributes such as skin, hair and eye color, there are also tendencies to sin that are transmitted from parents to child. In conception, attributes of both father and mother are focused in the *zygote* formed by the union of male and female *gametes*. Through genetic coding, ancestral nature passes from generation to generation. Not all the weaknesses of the flesh of ancestors are manifested in every person born. Nevertheless, every person is a carrier of unseen tendencies.

These tendencies may not be manifested in one generation, but may and do crop up after several generations to plague an individual or a family in various ways as they are given in to, as for example, in the case of David.

Weakened tendencies to sin, received and cultivated by David's forefathers, were passed on by him and were inherited by Jesus. That is the significance of the phrase about Jesus in that He was "the seed of David according to the flesh" (Romans 1:3). However, unlike David, Jesus did not succumb to the infirmities of His inherited fallen human nature. Deeply touched by them, yes, but He "condemned" them where they reside and ruled in the flesh (Romans 8:3). The Savior of the world chose to enter into the hereditary line of David—the line that was the most degraded and corrupted of the twelve tribes of Israel. And He conquered all the corruptions of the flesh. He overthrew the enemy's stronghold entirely. He invaded enemy-held territory and was completely victorious.

Christ was born holy, lived a holy life, and returned to heaven as spotless as when from there He came. But that holiness was lived in fallen human nature by the power of the Holy Spirit. He depended solely and totally upon that power. Christ was righteous by faith, not by human nature. His sinlessness was in character and in life, while living in fallen flesh. There is no evidence that Christ had holy human flesh.

Stephen Haskell, writing at the turn of the last century, combated a doctrine that emerged within several Christian groups. He dealt with it in one of those groups. The end result of that false doctrine was this: the only way a person could overcome sin was to have a change from inherited fallen human nature to a holy nature like that possessed by Adam before he fell. This experience was based on the hypothesis that Christ took Adam's sinless human nature and so by-passed the law of heredity and the consequent struggles of the rest of the fallen race. The advocates of the so-called "holy flesh" doctrine claimed that Christ was exempt from the working of the great law of heredity. Overcoming, to some of those advocates of one hundred years ago, meant receiving so-called "holy flesh." Haskell addressed this issue with one group of people involved in what was called "The Holy Flesh Movement."

He wrote an editorial entitled, "Christ in Holy Flesh, or a Holy Christ in Sinful Flesh." His employment of alternate propositions marked the specific stage when rival doctrines about Christ's human nature were being advanced for consideration. The entire article was devoted to "A Holy Christ in Sinful Flesh." The alternate hypothesis was, as stated above, that Christ was sinless because He took "holy flesh," the sinless nature of Adam in his pre-fall state. That which especially caught my attention in the editorial was when Haskell quoted Psalm 51:5 and then commented, "It was Christ through David who said: 'Behold I was shapen in iniquity; and in sin did my mother conceive me.' This states plainly the nature of the humanity in which Christ was conceived." Stephen Haskell, *The Review and Herald*, October 2, 1900. And it was in this nature that Christ condemned and overcame sin. It is this that gives us hope.

Christ, though innocent of any personal sin, took His place before the throne of grace as a penitent. Psalm 51 does not speak about the dignity of His birth, as descended from the prince of the tribe of Judah. It deals with hereditary tendencies to sin, along with the committed sins of the world that were laid upon Jesus.

Christ had such a deep sense of sin that He continually thought of it with sorrow of heart and shame. He was mortified and humbled by it. He "learned obedience by the things that He suffered." Christ submitted to the discipline of a penitent. There is but one law of repentance for the fallen race, and Christ came under that law. His confession is specific. His conscience smote Him. Not for any personal sin of His own, mind you, but for your sins and mine.

## Christ laments in this passage.

Sin was committed against God. God was wronged. Sin denies this truth. It was God's command that was disobeyed, His manner of life that was despised, His name dishonored, His promise distrusted. God is treated deceitfully and disingenuously by sin. And Christ bore it and felt it all as though He had committed the sins of the whole world.

Christ, as Representative of the fallen race, walked in the way of righteousness. That way is the way of repentance, faith and obedience. He fulfilled all righteousness.

Christ's repentance was unto death. When we repent, we die to sin. When Christ repented, He died because of our sin. He was made to be sin itself for us (2 Corinthians 5:21). Treated as the number one sinner, treated as fallen Adam deserved to be treated, treated as the fallen race merits, Christ suffered the full consequences of the fall. He died the death of the damned.

Nearly the whole of Psalm 51 deals with the awfulness of sin, repentance and confession from which Christ was not exempt. Over-shadowed by the Holy Spirit, Mary conceived and gave birth to that holy Child Jesus (Luke 1:30-35). Christ was born holy. He lived a holy life by faith, and died holy, wholly in faith. Upon His ascension to heaven He was as holy as when He descended in condescension to His lowly birth in the stable. But He was conceived in fallen flesh. Mary, fallen by human nature, could only pass on that same nature to Jesus. It was impossible for her to give to Him a higher, holier, sinless nature than she had.

The Spirit of Christ moved upon David to write concerning Himself, "Behold, I was shapen in iniquity, and in sin did my mother conceive me" (Psalm 51:5). Some may counter this concept with the fact that David was writing about his own inherited human nature, which he received from his mother. And that is true. It is likewise true of all the rest of the human family. And Jesus shared with us in our common lot. He entered into His own creation through the law of heredity. His was a miraculous conception. But miracles do not ignore or destroy God's natural laws. A miracle is never an exemption or a transgression. If a law is valid, there is no need for an exemption. An exemption is wrong. If an exemption is needed, the law is wrong.

**Christ came to us where we are.**

He is not afar off, but nigh unto us. He became "us." And He became "us" in the same way that we became—through conception and birth through the genetic working of the great law of heredity. Jesus was the seed of David. Paul wrote that this is the good news, the glad tidings, the gospel (Romans 1:1-3). Christ was the fruit of David's body (Psalm 132:10, 11).

It is written, "From this man's [David's] seed, according to the promise, God raised up for Israel a Savior—Jesus" (Acts 13:23). The good news of the gospel is that Christ, the Savior of the world, was born of the seed of David according to the flesh. Carried through the genes is the DNA coding that transmits fallen nature from one generation to the next. Jesus, the second Adam came through David and Abraham all the way back to the first Adam. Christ was born "according to the flesh." There has been only one kind of human flesh born and that is fallen. The fallen flesh or nature of Adam reached all the way to the flesh of Jesus. It reached Him through the family line of David.

Christ came with such a heredity that enters into and shares our sorrows and temptations. The results of the working of the law of heredity of the humanity of Christ are revealed to us in the names of His ancestors as recorded in Matthew 1.

Satan, knowing that Christ must come through this royal line, especially targeted it. He corrupted it. Christ coming in the flesh came into the flesh in the weakest of families. This reveals Christ's willingness to be the Savior of the world. No one needs to think that Christ does not understand him because of heredity or environmental limitations. He is touched with the feelings of our weaknesses. He is a complete Savior, both from the temptations from without and those from within our fallen nature.

# Chapter 12

# The Seed of David

# Psalm 132:11

U nder the solemnity of an oath that would not be an-
nulled, God promised to David a descendant to sit
upon his throne. The oath reads: "The Lord has sworn
in truth to David; He will not turn from it: 'I will set upon your
throne the fruit of your body.'" There are those who believe
this psalm was written by Solomon and was to be sung at
the dedication of the temple in Jerusalem. Be that as it may,
Peter applies this verse to Christ. More than applying it to
Christ, Peter states unequivocally that David himself knew
this promise was about Christ: "Therefore, being a prophet,
and knowing that God had sworn with an oath to him, that of
the fruit of his loins, according to the flesh, he would raise up
Christ to sit on his throne" (Acts 2:30).

Christ was in the loins of David genetically when the
promise was given to him. To illustrate, consider Hebrews 7:9,
10: Levi, the great-grandson of Abraham, was in his loins when
at that time Abraham was childless. Levi was in Abraham
genetically. So the human nature Christ inherited was from
David.

Paul, while at Antioch in Pisidia, preached to the Jews
that from David's "seed, according to the promise, God raised
up for Israel a Savior—Jesus" (Acts 13:23). The word "seed" in
the language used by Paul is *spermatos,* from which our Eng-

lish word *sperm* comes. The sperm of David was the reproductive cell by which the traits of his human nature were passed on from one generation to the next down to the humanity that Christ would inherit from His own mother, Mary.

Consider briefly the design and function of sperm. Within the sperm are chromosomes—threadlike linear strands of DNA and associated proteins in the nucleus of the cell that carry the genes and which serve in the transmission of hereditary information.

Within the chromosomes is located the "recipe" for our hereditary traits. A gene is a hereditary unit that occupies a specific location on a chromosome and determines a particular characteristic in an organism. Transmitted from parent to offspring are the colors of skin, eye and hair, and all other physical characteristics. Hereditary mental and moral weaknesses are likewise transmitted through the genes. However, genetic tendencies to sin are not to be construed as excuses for bad conduct.

That which is inherited through birth is termed nature. Mental and moral limitations, which enfold man without conscious volition, are part of this legacy. The physical structure with its established tendencies, received from previous generations, is included in this legacy. Heredity is the law of transmission. You and I are everything that our ancestors contributed and delivered to us mentally, morally and physically at conception, combined with prenatal influences up to the time of birth. We all, without exception, were born with a fallen human nature inherited from our parents and the rest of our ancestors, reaching all the way back to Adam and Eve.

Our first parents were created with sinless natures. All their tendencies were toward goodness and purity. It was in their nature to be and to do good. Had they remained faithful to God, their offspring, through the law of heredity would have inherited only righteous tendencies. But because of their sin, all of their offspring without exception were and are born with tendencies to sin. Adam, Abraham and David could not give to any of their descendants a higher nature than they possessed.

## Some persons blame "bad genes" for their sins.

Included here would be alcoholism and homosexuality. Genes can predispose one person to getting drunk more readily than another person, but those genes do not force that person to drink alcohol. The same principle applies with regard to homosexuality. Genes may give some males fewer androgens (steroid hormones that develop and maintain masculine characteristics) than others, but those genes do not make anyone engage in homosexual behavior. Nor does a limited number of androgens cause that kind of conduct.

In writing to the Corinthians, Paul stated: "I keep under my body" (1 Corinthians 9:27). He recognized that if his body was not kept under control, its hereditary claims would make unreasonable claims. The inherited desires and impulses and passions were severely disciplined by the power of God in cooperation with his choices. The flesh, or fallen nature, is to be "crucified with all its affections and lusts." This is accomplished only by the grace of God in putting to death the temptations to sin that come from within our hereditary make-up. Every thought, every desire, every impulse, is to be brought into "captivity" to Christ. His life becomes the vitalizing power in the life of the believer, and thus the temptations that assail us from within and from without are resisted and overcome.

Full of significance are the words, "from [David's] seed, according to the promise, God raised up for Israel a Savior—Jesus" (Acts 13:23). Paul in his introduction to Romans takes up this same thought and presents Christ as "born of the seed of David according to the flesh" as "the gospel of God" (Romans 1:1-3). The gospel is the good news about the genealogy of Jesus. Not only is this a great theological truth. It is also a most comforting thought for frail, erring mortals. God's power was manifest in our human heredity, in Christ, when He became incarnate. This is the good news—the gospel of God.

The New Testament introduces us to Jesus through His genealogy (see Matthew 1:1-17). This is "the book of the generation of Jesus Christ, the son of David, the son of Abraham." David had all the passions of fallen human nature through the law of heredity. We will take a brief look at the ancestry and the posterity of David. This is the line from which Christ came as to His human nature. Concentrated in Christ were all the weaknesses of humanity, especially of the line of David from the family of Judah. The fact of Christ's fight of faith and consequent victory gives hope and comfort to mortals weakened and bowed down with hereditary weaknesses.

Of the men mentioned by Matthew, several were extremely wicked: Jacob—selfish, crafty, deceitful; Judah—a man of licentious conduct, whose children were born of an impure woman (see Genesis 38); David—an adulterer and a murderer; Solomon and later Manasseh, brought into Israel the idolatrous worship of Molech (the national deity of the Ammonites who offered their children in sacrifice to him. Manasseh practiced this abomination. See 2 Kings 21:6). Ahaz was a leader in apostasy. Of Rehoboam, Abijam, Jehoram, Amon, and other kings of Judah, the record is about the same. Some of these men had not one redeeming trait in their characters.

At one time the royal line was nearly eliminated by Ahab and Jezebel's daughter. Joash, the last rightful heir to the throne, as a baby was hidden in the temple for six years. (2 Kings 11:1-3; 2 Chronicles 22:10-12). Satan knew that Christ would have to come through this line. Thus he moved the worshippers of Baal to try to destroy the royal line of Judah. Having failed to destroy it, he proceeded to corrupt it. Although Judah's descendants ruled in Israel and later in the kingdom of Judah, they lost all ability to control themselves. Notwithstanding that they were kings, they were the weakest of the weak, morally. This was the royal line of Judah. Royal, but royal rogues! From such an ancestry Jesus came.

Search His ancestry for a Daniel, an Isaiah, an Elijah, a Moses, or a Jeremiah. They are not there. They are conspicuously absent.

There are four women (other than Mary) mentioned in Matthew's account of the genealogy of Jesus. Of the four, two were adulteresses, Tamar and Bathsheba. One was a harlot, Rahab. Ruth the Moabitess was from a race that was the offspring of incest between Lot and his oldest daughter (see Genesis 19:30-38). From such an ancestry Jesus came. He chose to come from such an ancestry.

**Can you fathom such love as this?**

Truly, Christ became one of us. Mary was not an "incubator," she was His *mother*. And He is not ashamed to call us "brethren." This should give us all encouragement regardless of the hereditary background from which we originate, and of which we had no choice.

God, by an oath to David, swore that from his loins must come Christ, the Messiah, the Savior of man. David was given the gospel in that oath concerning Christ as the fruit of his body, as recorded in Psalm 132:11. That good news continues to ring in our ears as we hear it. God was morally and ethically bound to send His Son to the lost human race in order to save it. Christ came and fought and conquered sin in our nature. "In all things it behooved Him to be made like unto His brethren, that He might be a merciful and faithful High Priest in things pertaining to God, to make reconciliation for the sins of the people. For in that He Himself hath suffered being tempted, He is able to succor them that are tempted" (Hebrews 2:17,18). Because He "was in all points tempted like as we are, yet without sin" we may know that He is "touched with the feelings of our infirmities" (Hebrews 4:15, 14).

Whether we are weakened by ancestral infirmities or with sins that we have habitually practiced, we can know that we have a complete Savior. He, burdened with inherited weaknesses, was also weighted down with the committed sins of the world. These were all placed upon Him. Having never sinned, yet He knows what we go through. And He knows just how much divine power we need when we are tempted for He received power from on high, by faith, while He walked this earth as a man.

# Chapter 13

## Justice and Mercy Meet in Christ
## Psalm 85:10

"Mercy and truth have met together; righteousness and peace have kissed each other."

In this verse we have a figure of speech called "personification," by which the attributes of God are represented as actions of human beings. In this we observe the harmony of God's divine attributes in Christ's undertaking of our salvation.

Because of Christ's work, God shows mercy upon the fallen race without violating His truth and justice. In Him mercy and truth are met together, righteousness and peace kiss each other. Separated for a time, now joined, they are at-one in Him. Christ as Mediator not only brought heaven and earth, God and man, together. He also joined together forever the divine attributes of God.

Some persons dwell on God's mercy but not His justice. Others focus the attention on the justice of God to the neglect of His mercy. At times we are apt to lose sight of either or both of these prerogatives. However, we must keep in mind that God is infinite in every perfection. A prerogative is a right or power belonging to a person by virtue of rank, position or character.

God's prerogatives of justice and mercy are equal in rank and authority. They are clothed with imperative power.

Both have a right to require and demand priority. These prerogatives we will consider in this chapter.

### Justice and mercy are twins, but not identical.

They are not one and the same. Each has an identity of its own. Lucifer (later became known as Satan), the angel who sinned and defected from the government of God, challenged God's justice and mercy. Sin brought questions to the minds of all intelligent creatures in the universe concerning the prerogatives of justice and mercy during the war of the universe between God and Lucifer.

From the beginning of the controversy, Lucifer was at odds with God's moral law (see John 8:44, 45; Isaiah 14:12-14). Because justice and mercy are foundational to the government of God and therefore to His law, conflict arose concerning the pardon of sin. If justice should be found inconsistent with mercy, it would be impossible for sinners to be forgiven. If God's law should be broken, then every violation of it must be punished. And if mercy should be extended, God would not be a God of justice and of truth. From legal proceedings in our own day we observe that Satan's purpose has been to divorce mercy from justice.

After making man in His image, God carefully and specifically informed Adam about the single forbidden tree placed in the garden of Eden (Genesis 2:9, 16, 17). Lucifer knew that in some manner the prerogative of justice had to be revealed to man. He knew well the attributes of God. He knew that God's government must stand by virtue of the unity of the prerogatives of God, and accordingly, that it must fall by separating these same prerogatives.

The great mastermind of evil knew God better than any other created being. He knew where and how to strike a telling blow against God. Attributes most despised by Lucifer are the prerogatives of truth, justice and mercy. These he was compelled to assault.

Lucifer thought that if God should exercise any one of His prerogatives, others would have to be set aside. He reasoned that if justice should be exercised, then mercy would have to go. But if mercy should be exhibited, then truth and justice would be denied.

The enemy of God and man laid well his plans. That which worked in heaven was now set into motion against Adam.

Step one: through the medium of influence of mind upon mind he enticed Eve to sin.

Step two: Eve in turn by the same principle of mind influencing mind, led Adam into sinning against God's express command.

Step three: thus Lucifer hoped to create a gulf between the sovereign prerogatives of truth, justice and mercy.

Consider this scenario of the personification of God's prerogatives in relation to Himself after sin entered the human race:

Truth: Is it not true that You fixed a punishment for man if he should disobey? If You are true, You are obligated to follow that which is true.

Mercy: If You are merciful, You must have mercy on fallen man. If You can have no mercy on him, You cannot be called merciful.

Justice: Are You not called just and righteous? If You are just, You will exercise punishment on the transgressor. If You do not, You cannot be just.

**Peace fled from the heart of God.**

Through sin Satan succeeded in separating not only man from God, but also the prerogatives of the justice and mercy of God. There is nothing in the universe by which finite minds can compare the rending of the divine attributes within God Himself. Satan thought the gulf separating justice and mercy could not be spanned.

With an intensity that defies description, both fallen and unfallen beings watched the unfolding of the principles of truth, justice and mercy in man's redemption.(1 Peter 1:10-12). Angels studied into the significance of the sacrificial system established after man fell. Later, when the tabernacle was built in the wilderness, they studied that earthly typical sanctuary and its services. The mercy seat covered the ark that enshrined the tables of the law. Here was foreshadowed Christ, the mysterious Mercy-seat of God. Here God was revealed. He was revealed as both just to His law and as the justifier of the repenting, believing sinner (Romans 3:25, 26; Hebrews 2:17; 1 John 4:10).

It took nothing less than the cross of Calvary to settle the question raised by sin. The cross was the mysterious medium used by God to reconcile His own prerogatives. Not only man and God were drawn together by the death of Christ, but also justice and mercy. The cross alone was the bridge by which the gulf produced by sin could be spanned and thus the prerogatives of God could be reunited.

Paul caught a glimpse of the glory of the cross as on it Christ reconciled the things of heaven as well as those of earth:

> "It pleased the Father that in Him [Christ] all the fullness should dwell, and by Him to reconcile all things to Himself, by Him, whether things on earth or things in heaven, having made peace through the blood of the cross ... in the body of His flesh through death ..." (Colossians 1:19-22).

The agonizing, questioning cry of Christ, "My God, My God! Why have You forsaken Me?" echoed God's own breaking heart as He as well as Jesus felt the conflict between infinite emotions in the rending asunder of His own attributes of justice and mercy. This was part of the horrible experience of the atonement from God's standpoint in affliction. In all of Christ's affliction He was afflicted. Especially through the cross, Christ gave to man a new revelation of God. Yes, God and man were reconciled. But more than this, through the death of Christ justice and mercy within God's very being were at-one-ment also! Just before His committal prayer, Jesus made His last declaration, "It is finished" And as Justice approached the cross in reverent submission, Mercy echoed, "It is finished," and replied, "It is enough."

Thus through the cross, Christ reconciled "things in heaven"—the holy attributes of justice, and mercy and truth. When Christ was uplifted on the cross, He drew both justice and mercy across the gulf of separation. In Christ, God reconciled the world unto Himself; in Christ God reconciled His own attributes of justice and mercy.

Full of significance are the words of Christ when He said, "And I, if I be lifted up from the earth, will draw all to Myself" (John 12:32). (The word "men" is in italics to indicate that it was added.) Not only is man drawn to Jesus, but the very attributes of God are pulled across the gulf that sin produced. The devil's charges were proved to be false. God's government and His administration were found to be flawless. Justice and mercy and truth were vindicated and honored. One day Satan will bow down and concede and confess that the conflict he generated was forever settled beyond question.

Psalm 85:10, personifying God's attributes, reveals the work of the cross and sums up the healing process in the heart of God. "Mercy and truth are met together; righteousness [justice] and peace have kissed each other."

Because of Christ's work of reconciling the prerogatives of justice and mercy, each stand separate in all their exalted dignities, yet they are united. Because of the cross and the consequent reconciliation between the divine prerogatives, mercy becomes a terrible power to punish sin while justice demands forgiveness for all who believe. The believing sinner has a right, based on God's justice, to ask God to revive him and to deliver him from trouble. Because of mercy the Psalmist asked that his enemies be cut off:

"Revive me, O Lord, for Your name's sake! For Your righteousness' [justice's] sake bring my soul out of trouble. In Your mercy cut off my enemies,

and destroy all those who afflict my soul; for I am
Your servant" (Psalm 143:11, 12).

Compare that with the following proverbial saying
written by Solomon: "By mercy and truth iniquity is purged"
(Proverbs 16:6, KJV). On the one hand, God's mercy is involved not only in showing clemency, compassion and sympathy, but also in execution and in punishing sin. Justice, on the
other hand, is exercised in forgiveness and cleansing from sin.
It is because of justice that we have a right to a Savior. "If we
confess our sins, He is faithful and just to forgive us our sins
and to cleanse us from all unrighteousness" (1 John 1:9).

Man considers justice as the reason we should not be
pardoned, knowing we deserve to be punished. Justice must
be satisfied. But justice *has* been satisfied. Because of this,
justice has a royal right to declare forgiveness to anyone who
believes in Jesus as his Substitute and Savior. Rather than a
barrier to justification, the justice of God is the very ground
and reason for it. It is God's argument in our behalf. Notice
what Paul wrote concerning this:

"Being justified freely by His grace through the redemption that is in Christ Jesus, whom God set forth to be a
propitiation by His blood, through faith, to demonstrate His
righteousness [justice], because in His forbearance God had
passed over the sins that were previously committed, to demonstrate at the present time His righteousness [justice], that
He might be just and the justifier of the one who has faith in
Jesus" (Romans 3:24-26).

**Clearly, justification by faith rests on God's justice.**

Justification is an act of His justice. This is because
Christ exhausted the penalty of justice on our behalf, in our
stead, in our place. Then, when we believe, justice demands
our justification. We call for mercy, but justice answers. As a
just God, He cannot condemn the believer, since Christ dissi-
pated the sentence against us. The attribute that seemed both
to Satan and man to be the reason for God not to forgive is the
very basis for why He does pardon us through faith in Christ.

Because of the reconciliation of the divine prerogatives, compromise with sin is not allowed and the claims of justice are not ignored. Each attribute of God is given its ordained place. Mercy's clemency and compassionate character are not destroyed when mercy punishes sinful, impenitent man devoid of remorse who throws away God's gift of Christ to him. And without violating its integrity, justice is exercised in pardoning the repentant transgressor.

Through mercy Christ became a curse for us. Consequently, we have been redeemed from the curse, according to justice. Because of justice we have a right to claim Christ as our Savior. Because we are sinners we are entitled to come to Christ.

Like a flash of lightning, Satan and his accusations fell from the affections of the watching universe when the redemption price was paid.

## Since the cross of Christ, the devil has changed his tactics.

Now he claims that because of Christ's death, justice is set aside. The mercy and love of God are offered as his message to man, minus justice. Today many in Christianity are convinced that not only the penalty for sin was abolished, but also the justice of God. Mercy according to this doctrine distances itself from justice. But no, God's mercy manifested to mankind through Jesus does not set aside justice.

The last battle of the universe will be over the prerogatives considered in this chapter. Satan's claim that God's mercy destroyed justice at the cross has implications for us today. While he clothes God with his own tyrannical attributes, he advocates a sentimental love that veils the law, justice and retributive punishment. It matters not to Satan how he accomplishes his nefarious work. He needs confusion to establish himself. He attempts to amalgamate the meanings of justice and mercy into a single meaning when he cannot separate them.

God's message for the last days will present both justice and mercy. Each attribute will be allowed to stand distinct but united in their sovereign majesties. The meeting together—the linking—of these prerogatives means they are forever inseparable. In Christ, they are always found side by side in every situation.

# Chapter 14

## "Melchizedek: Priest-King"

## Psalm 110

Although this psalm is short, it is very deep and rich with Christ and His righteousness. It is pure unadulterated gospel. It is the truth as it is in Jesus. The subject spoken of here is without a doubt Christ. He applied it to Himself (see Matthew 22:44). Others also in the New Testament apply this passage to Christ (see Acts 2:34; Hebrews 1:13; 10:12.13).

There are several orders of priests recorded in the Old Testament. These include the Patriarchal, the Levitical, the Aaronic, and the Melchizedekal. Christ's priesthood was greater than all others combined. A single kind of priesthood could not sufficiently illustrate Christ's work on behalf of the fallen race. Of the mentioned priesthoods the Melchizedek order was the greatest of all (Hebrews 7:1-10). Melchizedek is mentioned historically only briefly and in passing in an account concerning Abraham (Genesis 14:18-20), but he is significantly mentioned in this psalm under consideration, and seven times in the book of Hebrews and is directly related to Christ and His priestly work (Psalm 110:4; Hebrews 5:6,10; 6:20; 7:11, 15, 17, 21).

The priesthood of Melchizedek links our day with the days of Abraham in that Christ's priesthood is after the order of Melchizedek's. The seventh chapter of Hebrews repeats the story of Melchizedek recorded in the fourteenth chapter of Genesis. The setting of the return of Abraham is from an expedition against several nations who had united together and in their conquests kidnapped Abraham's nephew Lot. Melchizedek met Abraham, blessed him, and gave him bread and wine to drink.

### Melchizedek was a high priest of God.

Abraham recognized that fact and gave to him a tenth part of the recovered spoil. The Melchizedek priesthood is the Christian priesthood of Christ. And those who are Christ's will give tithe of all their increase just as Abraham recognized the fact that the tithe belongs to the Lord.

Christ also blessed His disciples with bread and wine at His last supper. But more than just temporal blessings, the bread and wine were consecrated by Christ to represent His great sacrifice given for the fallen race that we might be blessed. And also the bread and wine represent the spiritual provisions Christ has stored up for us in the Everlasting Covenant of grace for our refreshment when we become weary with our spiritual conflicts. Christ our High Priest meets us in our spiritual battles, refreshes us, renews our strength and blesses us. As God sent Melchizedek to bless Abraham, so He sent Christ to bless us in turning us from our iniquities (Acts 3:26).

### Who was this priest, Melchizedek?

Some have thought that it must have been Christ in human form. Others speculate that he came from another planet. As to the first notion, no one can be a type of himself. There is a distinction to be made between a similitude and reality, shadow and substance, or else they are of the same identity which then destroys the type-antitype construction. Melchizedek was one of an order; Christ was "another priest" of the same order (Hebrews 7:15).

As to the second idea, priests were to be of the human family. A priest was to be beset with the infirmities of those whom he represented (Hebrews 5:1-5). It is in connection with the Melchizedek priesthood that it is written of Christ, "who in the days of His flesh, when He had offered up prayers and supplications, with vehement cries and tears to Him who was able to save Him from death, and was heard because of His godly fear, though He were a Son, yet He learned obedience by the things that He suffered" (Hebrews 5:6-8).

Melchizedek was a Canaanite Gentile ordained of God with the distinction as "priest of the Most High God" who bestowed God's blessing upon the Hebrew race in Abraham. He was a king of Gentiles and a priest of Gentiles, again typifying Christ. Christ was of both Gentile and Hebrew descent (see Matthew 1). His priesthood was greater than all in that it encompasses all mankind everywhere and in every place.

Christ became the King and Head and Mediator of the fallen race. He was/is the "Light to the Gentiles." He is "the Savior of every man, especially those who believe" (Isaiah 49:6; 1 Timothy 4:10). Like Melchizedek, Christ too was God's Priest among the Gentiles. The Gentiles must come to God through Him. It is only through this priesthood that we can obtain reconciliation and remission of sin.

As a type of Christ, Melchizedek was like Him. He "was made like unto the Son of God" (Hebrews 7:2). He was a type of Christ as a king and as a priest. The word "Melchizedek" is more of a title than a personal name. It is compounded from two words, Melek, which means a king from *malak,* to reign; and *zedek,* meaning righteousness. His title means "King of righteousness" and Salem, the name of his city-kingdom, means "peace" (Hebrews 7:3). Melchizedek not only was a priest of righteousness, he was also a king of righteousness and peace. Righteousness and peace belong together. When a person believes and is justified, at that very moment he is at peace with God. This is because righteousness and peace meet in Jesus. He is "the Lord our Righteousness" and the "Prince of Peace." The work of Christ's righteousness is peace, quietness and assurance forever (Romans 5:1; Jeremiah 21:6; Isaiah 9:6; 32:17).

Righteousness and peace come to us through the Melchizedek order. By that order we are saved. Christ is our King and Priest representing us upon the throne of the universe which is in God's temple in heaven. Our hope is based on this order of priesthood. It is centered in the fact that Christ our "forerunner is for us entered (within the veil of the heavenly temple), even Jesus," "made an high priest forever after the order of Melchizedek" (Hebrews 6:19, 20).

So far as the inspired written record goes, every king who attempted to unite the two offices of priest and king met with God's disapproval. However, both Melchizedek and Christ were appointed to those united offices by God, and Christ by oath. Melchizedek represented God to the people he governed, and he was their representative to Him. So with Christ. Of Him it is written, "The Lord has sworn and will not repent, 'You are a priest for ever according to the order of Melchizedek.'" "The Lord said to My Lord, 'Sit at My right hand, till I make Your enemies Your footstool'" (Psalm 110:4, 1).

Of Christ's kingly priesthood it is written, "He shall build the temple of the Lord. He shall bear the glory, and shall sit and rule on His throne; so shall He be a priest on His throne, and the counsel of peace shall be between them both" (Zechariah 6:13). As priest upon the Father's throne Christ makes reconciliation for the sins of the people. The power and authority by which He does so is the power of the throne of the universe, upon which He is seated at the right hand of the Father. It was by God's oath that Christ was made a High Priest after the order of Melchizedek.

The priesthood of Melchizedek was greater than the patriarchal in that Abraham, a patriarchal priest, paid tithe to him and knelt in submission to him, receiving the blessing of this person who was greater than himself.

Likewise, that priesthood was greater than the Aaronic because Aaron in Abraham paid tithe to Melchizedek and also received the Melchizedek benediction as Abraham knelt. And this was long before Aaron was born. This well illustrates the corporate solidarity of the human race.

We were all in Adam after as well as before he sinned. If he had perished in the garden of Eden the moment he sinned, you and I would not have seen the light of day for we were in his loins as was Levi in Abraham's. And further, if we were not in Christ when He died, we could not be saved. We all died, since Christ died for all (2 Corinthians 5:14). This illustrates the corporate, legal equivalent of the eternal death of the damned.

This priesthood and kingship of Christ are connected with God's oath. These offices of Christ came from God, ratified by His oath. This oath is God's assurance of His gift of Christ to mankind. This oath is more necessary than the food we eat and the water we drink and the air we breathe, for without it we would have nothing to eat, drink or breathe. God "swore and will not repent." To repent means basically to have a change of mind about something, or to turn back from a purpose. This gives force to the oath made by God. It is unchangeable, no matter what the cost to Him. He placed Himself at risk in this oath. He staked His throne for the fulfillment of His word.

This oath is security of the plan of redemption based on Christ in human nature. It was to be a terrible price at which that oath was to be fulfilled. The Father and the Son must be separated. The Son must give up forever some of His attributes as God, and take upon Himself the form and nature of the fallen race in order to save it. And in this condition Christ must meet the enemy and conquer him in behalf of mankind. He must meet and overcome Satan and his temptations on every point where the first Adam failed.

**More than this, Christ was to "taste death for every man" (Hebrews 2:9).**

And through the Father's infinite connection with Christ, He too would taste it in His Son. He drank the whole torrent of this world's sorrow.

This oath and God's determination not to turn aside from it involved Christ being "made to be sin for us, who knew no sin, that we might be made the righteousness of God in Him" (2 Corinthians 5:21). He was to be made sin itself in order to minister to us righteousness and peace. From this God would not turn aside, even though it cost the Godhead infinite sufferings. The occasion for repentance, for turning back, was the cost of our redemption. It was Christ or us, and the Godhead took the more costly route. They decided to pay the price, "for God so loved the world that He gave His only-begotten Son ..." (John 3:16). Whatever the combined forces of man and devils could throw at His Son, God would not withdraw from His settled purpose to make His Son a priest after the order of Melchizedek.

Included in the oath of the Melchizedek priesthood of Christ was Christ as the Surety of the everlasting covenant of God (Hebrews 7:20-22). Christ is the Surety of the everlasting covenant from two perspectives, that of man and that of God. A surety is a bondsman, a guarantor that a person will show up to answer charges of a complaint of guilt in a legal court hearing. If the person charged with the crime does not show up for the hearing, the bondsman forfeits what he put up as a guarantee. In the case of man, we failed and Christ forfeited His life. He made Himself responsible for our failure.

On the part of God He guaranteed the oath for our redemption. In behalf of God He paid the supreme sacrifice which is the basis of the everlasting covenant. You can read the covenant agreement between the Father and the Son in Isaiah 49. Christ was given to be a covenant to the people, for the people and of the people (Isaiah 49:8; see also 42:1-7).

A covenant is so called from the idea of sacrificing animals and passing between the divided parts in solemn covenant. This involved a promise and/or an oath that if one failed to perform his promise, then let him become like the dead divided carcasses through which he passed. God did this with Abraham. He gave to Abraham a promise, and backed it with an oath. And He did it with Christ and the human race. Adam lost his position and his possessions. Christ, the second

Adam, regained the lost dominion through the Melchizedek priesthood, by the oath of God.

The ministry of Christ in the heavenly sanctuary as our High Priest after the order of Melchizedek is for the specific and definite purpose of establishing the "better covenant" with its "better promises" in behalf of the "heirs of promise." Involved in the everlasting covenant is the restoration of the earth as an everlasting possession based on God's righteousness received by the inheritors through faith (Romans 4:13).

The carrying out of the oath of God in the covenant necessitated Christ being born into mortal flesh in order to die. It had to have been the nature of fallen man, because Adam in holy flesh could not die. This too was an occasion for God to turn aside. How could He allow His Son to become a part of the fallen race? He would do whatever it must take to redeem mankind. He swore that He would do it and would not turn away from His purpose. Christ would become one with the race. He would be numbered with the transgressors in order to save them. Christ for us, Christ with us, Christ as us. This was included in the order of the Melchizedek priesthood by the oath of God, notwithstanding that it would cause the greatest possible sorrow and suffering to the Father as well as to the Son.

Christ would, as the head of the fallen body of mankind, suffer with each member of His body till their suffering should cease forever and the power of sin over them be crushed forever. He is the Head of every man and it is when sin is eradicated that every tear shall be wiped away (1 Corinthians 11:3; Revelation 21:4). This includes the tears of God. His heart grieves while the body of Christ, the human race as well as the church, suffers.

There are seven New Testament references to Psalm 110:1 (Matthew 22:44; Mark 12:36; Luke 20:42; Acts 2:34; 1 Corinthians 15:25; Hebrews 1:13; 10:13). These refer to Christ's reign with His Father on His throne. There is one reference to His own reign upon His own throne (Revelation 3:21). Christ overcame, by faith, all opposition to be seated upon His Father's throne. His enemies were formidable. They were Satan and his combined host along with man, sin, guilt and death. Christ overcame all by faith while He lived. "Of the increase of His government and peace there will be no end" (Isaiah 9:6, 7).

In answer to Pilate's question, "Are you a king then?" Jesus replied, "To this end was I born" (John 18:37). Christ had to be "fitted" to be King of the human family. That fitness could not have been accomplished if He came only as the Son of God. To become the race's king He must come as the Son of Man. And this fitness had to be adapted to the requirements of the race who in the weakness of their human infirmities endured the fierce assaults and conflicts with sin and Satan. He must take upon Himself human nature and pass triumphantly through all the experiences of the subjects of His kingdom, taking their sins, but without sinning. He was born to be this kind of King.

Christ had to become the Seed of the woman before He could be our High Priest. This is so, because a Priest must be taken from among His brethren so that they can know that He is "touched with the feelings of their infirmities" (Genesis 3:15; Hebrews 2:17, 18; 4:15). Christ had to become the Seed of the woman to become our King, for it takes kingly authority rather than priestly power to bruise the serpent's head. Christ must be born *into* the human family. He was born to take fallen Adam's place. In taking his place, He became the King over all the earth and took the title conferred upon Him by the oath of God as Priest-King after the order of Melchizedek. God was morally obligated by His oath to make Christ a Priest-King. And Christ was under that same obligation in order to redeem us.

The term "right hand" denotes God's authority and highest power. Here it is used of the place and position accorded Christ in His human nature as now exalted. "Under His feet" is used to denote complete subjection to that highest power. Christ's enemies will become part of His footstool literally when they are reduced to the physical material of which the earth is composed. The earth is God's footstool and the wicked will become non-sentient ashes (Isaiah 66:1; Malachi 4:1, 3). The oath will reach its full effect when Christ takes possession of His kingdom in the earth made new.

**But it is in the here and now that Christ is making up the subjects for His kingdom.**

He takes people with various hereditary and cultivated backgrounds from every nation, kindred and tribe and transforms them into willing and obedient subjects in His present kingdom of grace. When He returns for His subjects He will translate them into His kingdom of glory. There they shall meet with the Father Himself and see His face and hear His words. They shall see Him who would not turn from His purpose to redeem them regardless of the cost to Himself. And as Melchizedek blessed God when he blessed Abraham, so the redeemed of the ages will voice the written words of John:

"Blessing and honor and glory and power
Be to Him who sits on the throne,
And to the Lamb, forever and ever!"
(Revelation 5:13).

# Chapter 15

# The Cornerstone

# Psalm 118: 22, 23

"The stone which the builders rejected has become the chief cornerstone. This was the Lord's doing; it is marvelous in our eyes."

Jesus referred to this prophecy toward the end of His life on earth (see Matthew 21:42). By a series of illustrations He revealed to the leaders of Israel what they were about to do in rejecting and putting Him to death. He finished His discourse by quoting Psalm 118:22, 23, and concluded that the kingdom of God would be taken from them and given to a nation that should bear the fruits of the kingdom.

Christ tried by every means within the range of His influence to make plain to His rejecters the nature of the foul deed they were about to do. He, the Cornerstone of the plan of salvation, was rejected by those who should have built their own characters, by faith, upon that solid Rock. Christ attempted to show them their danger by calling their attention to this prophecy of Psalm 118.

The prophecy of the rejected stone was an actual occurrence in Israel's history when they built the temple in Jerusalem. The workers took foundation stones from a quarry and moved them to the temple site. At the quarry the stones were measured and cut to exact size. Each stone was exactly fitted for the foundation before placement. When the workers brought the stones to the temple site they placed them in their proper positions without hammer or chisel (see 1 Kings 5:17, 18; 6:7).

One stone transported to the building site did not fit because of its size and unusual shape. Because of this, it was not accepted by the workers. It became an annoyance to them, always in their way. That rejected stone lay there in their way for a length of time.

Finally, when the workers came to lay the cornerstone, they could not find the right one to use. Ignoring the rejected stone, they searched for one that could bear the immense weight and pressure of the temple to be built upon the foundation. The proper stone must be used, for the wrong one would endanger the entire building. None of the chosen stones withstood the rigorous tests brought to bear upon them. Some crumbled from massive weights placed on them. Sudden atmospheric changes destroyed the stability of others.

Eventually attention was called to the stone the workers previously rejected and currently stumbled over. They saw it, but not really. The stone was a nuisance, and it never dawned on the workers that that stone was of any use whatever. However, while examining it, builders could find not one crack in it from exposure to the elements of weather. Next, in applying the pressure of great weights to the stone, those builders learned that it did not crumble. So the long rejected stone was now brought to the crucial location where the head or cornerstone was to be placed in the foundation. It was found to be an exact fit.

Isaiah wrote of Christ and applied the experience of the rejected stone to Him. The Spirit of prophecy spoke through him and he wrote: "Behold, I lay in Zion a stone for a foundation, a tried stone, a precious cornerstone, a sure foundation; whoever believes will not act hastily" (Isaiah 28:16). Earlier he wrote, "He will be ... a stone of stumbling and a rock of offense to both the houses of Israel, as a trap and a snare to the inhabitants of Jerusalem. And many among them shall stumble; they shall fall and be broken, be snared and taken" (Isaiah 8:14, 15). God, the Master builder of His spiritual temple of believers, laid the Cornerstone even though the builders rejected and stumbled over Him.

Paul used the experience of the rejected stone to illustrate the differences between the messages of righteousness by faith and righteousness by the works of the law. He wrote that

"the Gentiles, who did not pursue righteousness, have attained to righteousness, even the righteousness of faith; but Israel, pursuing the law of righteousness, has not attained to the law of righteousness. Why? Because they did not seek it by faith, but as it were by the works of the law. For they stumbled at that stumbling stone. As it is written: "Behold, I lay in Zion a stumbling stone and rock of offense, and whoever believes on Him will not be put to shame" (Romans 9:30-33).

Christ and His righteousness have endured every test of pressure brought to bear. He carried the entire world's burden of grief and guilt. He never failed and never shall. Because He passed every test, we can build on the sure Foundation and never be disappointed. To those who believe, He is a precious and a sure foundation; but to those who disbelieve, He is a stone of stumbling and a rock of offense.

In His earthly life and even to this day, Christ has borne neglect and abuse. He was, and is, "despised and rejected of men, a man of sorrows and acquainted with grief: ... He was despised and we esteemed Him not" (Isaiah 53:3). Men still slight His mercy, spurn His righteousness and despise His goodness. But He is the true Cornerstone, notwithstanding stumbling, bumbling, unbelief. Those who build on any foundation other than Christ will be swept away when the tempests of human passion in the last days of earth explode and rage through every land. But those who know and appreciate Him, build on the only solid foundation. Peter stated it this way, concerning Christ the Cornerstone: there is no "salvation in any other, for there is no other name under heaven given among men by which we must be saved" (Acts 4:12). All who live forever must and will build upon Christ the true and sure foundation.

"Coming to Him as to a living stone, rejected indeed by men, but chosen by God and precious, you also, as living stones, are being built up a spiritual house, a holy priesthood, to offer up spiritual sacrifices acceptable to God through Jesus Christ" (1 Peter 2:4, 5).

"Now, therefore, you are no longer strangers and foreigners, but fellow citizens with the saints and members of the household of God, having been built on the foundation of the apostles and prophets, Jesus Christ Himself being the chief cornerstone, in whom the whole building, being joined together, grows intro a holy temple of the Lord, in whom you also are being built together for a habitation of God in the Spirit" (Ephesians 2:19-22).

In His humiliation, Christ is the Stone of righteousness cut out of the mountain without hands. He is the Cornerstone of strength and firmness and duration and life eternal in the spiritual temple of the living God. He is a Cornerstone most precious. "This is marvelous in our eyes" (Psalm 118:23).

# The Love Song

# Psalm 45

This psalm is known as the Marriage or Love Song. It points to Messiah the Prince as the Royal Bridegroom, and to His church as His bride. The first half of the psalm reveals Christ as a Warrior and Bridegroom; the second half speaks about His bride.

The Spirit of Prophecy gave this song to David to write concerning Christ. David's heart burning within Him, motivated by the flame of love, wrote of love and of war. Although David says he will write of things pertaining to the king (perhaps himself), He directs his thoughts to Christ. He writes of the excellencies of Jesus: "You are fairer than the sons of men; grace is poured upon Your lips; therefore God has blessed You for ever" (Psalm 45:2). Christ is the favorite of heaven. Yet for our sake He became one of us. Because He is blessed for ever, so are we. He has the blessing, and He has it for us. We are blessed with all spiritual blessings in heavenly places in Christ (Ephesians 1:3).

Grace was poured into Christ's lips. Grace was given that He might know how to speak a word in season to those who are weary. The Father awakened Him morning by morning that He might be instructed in what to say and how to say it (Isaiah 50:4). From that grace came those gracious words that spoke to and blessed those who heard (Luke 4:22).

Not only was grace poured into His lips, but it was poured into His heart for strength and encouragement. Grace kept and qualified Jesus for His work as Savior and Mediator. And from His fullness of grace, we receive (John 1:16).

The Bridegroom is a Man of war who is victorious over all His enemies (Psalm 45:3-5). He comes to the field of battle to rescue His bride-to-be. She being in captivity needs to be set free before He can marry her. She, being in captivity to Satan and to self, needs to be delivered. Christ does it by the power of the "sword," which is His word. There is a sense in which even she must be conquered. She must be submissive to her Heavenly Husband. He is to be the head of the household of faith. The converting and controlling power of His word must capture her heart. There must be a willing obedience on her part, controlled by her appreciation of Him. In other words, she must learn to love Him. It does not come naturally.

The cause in which Christ is engaged is that of truth, meekness and righteousness (verse 4). These are the principles of His character that were lost by man. These Christ came to retrieve and rescue and to restore within His bride that she might be all glorious within. He proposes to do this with the everlasting gospel in these last days (Revelation 14:6-12).

Because Christ is the truth, and is meek and righteous, it is from Him that His spouse learns meekness that she might be clothed in His righteousness. Because of these, she shall prosper and stand by His side as His bride. But first His word must be allowed to work in her heart. The word sets up truth within her heart to rectify her mistakes; meekness to control her passions; righteousness to control her heart, and consequently her life.

Before the word can do its work within the heart of His bride-to-be, the arrows of conviction must penetrate her hardened conscience and fasten there with the piercing sharpness of the granite point of the arrow, and bring her to her true condition. She must be startled by her condition and then be brought into loving submission to the Man-of-war, the Bridegroom, the One who truly loves her.

Psalm 45:6, 7 are quoted in Hebrews 1:8, 9. From this we learn that it is God the Father who says to the Son in this psalm, "Thy throne O God, is for ever and ever: the sceptre of thy kingdom is a right sceptre" (KJV). Our Mediator, the Son of Man, is God. His kingdom is eternal, and He shall rule on this earth forever. All the opposition from the gates of hell shall not prevail against Him. His rulership is one of righteousness. Whatever Christ does, He will never wrong a single subject of His kingdom. He loves righteousness and He loves to do righteousness. He hates wickedness and He will eventually eradicate it from the universe where righteousness shall reign in every heart and in every place. And that work of righteousness is peace and assurance forever (Isaiah 32:15; Romans 5:1).

Christ was anointed with the oil of gladness. He was anointed above all others, whether they are kings or priests or even angels. The Spirit of God was given to Him without measure to qualify and to enable Him for His work. He came to preach and to deliver the captives (Isaiah 61:1; 11:2). Christ was filled with the oil of gladness, He delighted to carry out the work He was sent to do. Even the horribleness of the cross was endured for the joy that was set before Him, which joy was in seeing men and women, boys and girls, in His kingdom forever because they respond to His unconditional pursuing love (Hebrews 12:2). He is satisfied with the travail of His soul (Isaiah 53:11). The salvation of sinners is His joy. The holy angels rejoice over the salvation of sinners (Luke 15:10), but Christ's joy is even greater.

Notice His robes of state as they are described in Psalm 45:8. They are not depicted in terms of the pomp of purple, gold and silver. His robes are not for decoration. They are noted for their pleasantness. They smell of myrrh, aloes and cassia. These elements were compounded both in the oil and in the incense of the sanctuary. Both represented Christ's righteousness—the incense representing His robe of righteousness by which He justifies and clothes us, the oil representing the Holy Spirit of righteousness by which He anoints and sanctifies us.

The character developed in Christ during His lifetime on earth is represented by the making of the incense. Just as the typical priests in days of old put the ingredients of the incense together to offer as a sweet smelling offering in behalf of the people whom they represented, so did Christ in reality. Both the oil and the incense were so sacred that no one was to make anything that resembled or smelled like them (see Exodus 30:23-38). The lesson from the symbols is that there is no place in God's plan for our salvation for any merit on our part, or for any counterfeit righteousness that may resemble Christ's. No merit accrues from man. It is Christ only. Only Christ and His righteousness. And those who are clothed with His righteousness will proclaim that all encompassing subject. It will swallow up every other.

His ointment, His incense, draws souls to Himself, and this makes Him precious in their sight (Song of Solomon 1:3, 4; 1 Peter 2:7). Out of heaven's "ivory palaces" there wafts to earth the fragrance of Christ's righteousness. This fragrance is enjoyed by His followers on earth. Every good thing done by the believer is surrounded and made acceptable by this cloud covering of righteousness. Christ is "all and in all" (Colossians 3:11).

Psalm 45:9 depicts the church as His queen standing by His side. By an everlasting covenant He has betrothed this woman to Himself. She stands at His right hand, the place of honor. She is seen clothed in a garment woven with gold thread, even the gold of Ophir, the most pure and precious and valuable on earth. This is Christ's bride. This is the Lamb's wife. His graces are her ornaments. In Revelation 19:8 they are compared to fine linen, clean and white. Both the linen here and the gold of Ophir represent the purity and the costliness of Christ's grace and righteousness by which we are clothed.

Although they are free, they are not cheap. They cost Christ everything. Heaven itself was not considered of more value than was the lost race. His form of God was not considered, by Himself, of more value than mankind. He laid aside His form as God to take upon Himself our nature to redeem us (Philippians 2:5-7). He will retain our redeemed nature forever.

Forever He is the Son of Man. We are indebted to Jesus forever for the costliness of the garments by which He clothes us.

To Him we owe our redemption. Our adorning is not because of corruptible things such as silver and gold and diamonds—the base things of earth, but to the precious blood of the Son of God. Even now He is knocking, ever knocking, at the door of His bride's heart, inviting her, counseling her to receive the gold tried in the fire, the white raiment, the anointing oil and the gift of repentance (Revelation 3:18-20)—this that she might stand at His side in honor clothed in the garment He prepared for such an occasion, even the garment of the fragrance "of myrrh, and aloes, and cassia, out of the ivory palaces." She too will be glad with the joy that makes the Bridegroom delighted.

The last part of the psalm is addressed to the royal bride-to-be. In verse ten she is counseled to consider what has been said, and to incline her ear to what He will say to her. Just as a man and his bride are to separate from friends and family in the earthly order of things when they marry in order to become one flesh, so it is in the heavenly wedding. Christ and His bride are to become one. Christ has eyes only for her. He waits patiently for her to have eyes only for Him. Christ submitted Himself to her level. "The Word became flesh and dwelt among us" (John 1:14). He came to dwell with us as "God with us" (Matthew 1:23). He became one of us. Christ gave up everything for His bride.

Now He longs to see that same kind of submission on the part of His bride to Himself. This is the only way the marriage can last for eternity. She must renounce all others and have desires only for Him in accordance with the law of marriage. He renounced all for her. Will she not respond in a favorable decision to Him?

She is not to retain her affection for the things of this earth. Neither is she to covet a return to them. When she responds to His love, she will realize the delight He has for her. He desires the beauty that will come to her as the result of responding to Him. He is concerned for this beauty. This is the beauty of character. His concern is that if she should turn again to her old ways, her beauty will become blemished. There is no place for an amalgamated religion. It must be pure and undefiled.

The bride, the church, is to be subject to Christ as the wife is to the husband. This is the reverence, the love and the honor of which Paul writes in His letter to the Ephesians (Ephesians 5:24-31). The husband is to love, cherish, and protect his wife as Christ does the church. The church in turn ought to cherish and love Him.

God who said to His Son, "Thy throne is forever and ever" now addresses the church who, because of being espoused to His Son, He now calls His daughter (Psalm 45:10, 13). She is "all glorious within" and covered with a garment of woven gold. As mentioned above, the gold is that which comes from Christ. It is the gold of faith that works by love and is tested in the fires of affliction (see Galatians 5:6; Revelation 3:18; 1 Peter 1:7). This is the faith that justifies and sanctifies and glorifies. This faith is always associated with Christ's righteousness given in justification and sanctification, which entitles and fits the bride for marriage to Christ. The glory within is seen without. The glory within is the character of Christ woven into the fabric of her character. God's glory is His mercy and graciousness, longsuffering, goodness and truth (Exodus 33:18, 19; 34:5, 6).

**God speaks of the honors He designed especially for His daughter.**

The riches of the universe are laid before her. Her wedding shall be celebrated with a great deal of honor and joy. She shall be brought into the palace of the King of the universe (Psalm 45:14, 15). Even now the inhabitants of the universe are on tiptoe. They await the coming of the bride to the King's palace and the wedding of all weddings.

In the completion of the mystical body, when the church, the Lamb's bride-to-be, responds to His love, He knocks at the door of her house and calls to her: "Open for Me, My sister (i.e.

spouse), My love, My dove, My perfect one." Then shall the longing of Christ be satisfied (Song of Solomon 5:1, 2; Revelation 3:20). Then will go out the invitation:

"Let us be glad and rejoice and give Him glory, for the marriage of the Lamb has come, and His wife has made herself ready. And to her it was granted to be arrayed in fine linen, clean and bright, for the fine linen is the righteousness of the saints. Then he said to me, 'Write blessed are those who are called to the marriage supper of the Lamb!'" (Revelation 19:7-9).

This will be the day of His wedding, "The day of the gladness of His heart" (Song of Solomon 3:11; 2:8). On that day He will break into singing just "as the bridegroom rejoices over the bride, so shall your God rejoice over you" (Isaiah 62:5). Yes, the singing Savior "will rejoice over thee with joy; He will rest in His love, He will joy over thee with singing" (Zephaniah 3:17, KJV). On that occasion God's paean (an expression of feeling by calling on others to rejoice) will be answered as His people from every nation, kindred, tongue and people break into rapturous praise as they unite with God in His song of rejoicing:

"Sing, O daughter of Zion! Shout, O Israel! Be glad and rejoice with all your heart, O daughter of Jerusalem! The Lord has taken away your judgments, He has cast out your enemy. The King of Israel, the Lord, is in your midst; You shall see disaster no more" (Zephaniah 3:14, 15).

Psalm 45 ends with unending praise. The praise of this marriage will be perpetual in the tribute of Christ, the Bridegroom for His bride, and in the admiration and appreciation she has for Him. "I will make your name to be remembered in all generations; therefore the people shall praise you forever and ever" (verse 18).

# Chapter 17

# In Summary and Conclusion

W e have considered some of the psalms about Jesus, Christ's experiences in humanity—His life, His temptations, His sufferings and His death, His resurrection from the grave, and His ascension to heaven. Christ is our High Priest after the order of Melchizedek. He is the second and last Adam, the Head of the fallen race. There is nothing that touches us that does not touch Him.

Christ crucified is the scarlet thread that binds the Book of Psalms into a whole. In the passages we studied in this book we entered into His thoughts and feelings as we beheld and listened to the Word prophetically given in the gospel psalms. This is only a beginning. There is much more. As it was said by the queen of Sheba concerning Solomon, "indeed the half was not told me," so it is with Christ.

The discovery of Jesus in the psalms (and in every other book of the Bible) is like the discovery of a vast continent reached by ship. First the beachhead in the sand and then onward in search of the treasures of the land. When it comes to the discovery and the study of Christ, we are still by the seaside in the sand. Eternity will open up for us "all the treasures of wisdom and knowledge" hidden in Him (Colossians

2:3). Here and now, in our study of Christ, our hearts open up to Him in appreciation and our lips utter, "Thanks be to God for His indescribable Gift!" (2 Corinthians 9:15).